Instant Skits
for
Children's Ministry

by John Duckworth

Group
Loveland, Colorado

Dedication

To all the loving children's workers whose perseverance has been an example

to me—including Jean Doty, Lelia Dvorak, B.J. and Lynda Slinger,

Marian Morton, and Sandy Ramsey.

Instant Skits for Children's Ministry

Copyright © 1999 John Duckworth

Visit our Web site: **www.grouppublishing.com**

Credits
Book Acquisitions Editor: Lori Haynes Niles
Editors: Debbie Gowensmith and Linda Anderson
Quality Control Editor: Jody Brolsma
Chief Creative Officer: Joani Schultz
Copy Editor: Alison Imbriaco
Art Director: Kari K. Monson
Cover Art Director: Jeff A. Storm
Cover Designer: Joy C. Holden
Computer Graphic Artist: Fred Schuth
Cover Illustrator: Tim O'Hara
Production Manager: Peggy Naylor

Library of Congress Cataloging-in-Publication Data
Duckworth, John (John L.)
    Instant skits for children's ministry / by John Duckworth.
      p.   cm.
    ISBN 0-7644-2095-X
     1. Drama in Christian education. 2. Christian education of children. 3. Children's plays, American.
     4. Christian drama, American.
    I. Title.
    BV1534.4.D8295   1999
    246'.72--dc21

                                    99-28529
                                    CIP

10 9 8 7 6 5 4   08 07 06 05 04 03 02 01

Printed in the United States of America.

Contents

Introduction

Welcome to the Skit Book for *Every* Children's Ministry!

Sure, skits are a great idea. They make learning active and visual. They build relationships as kids and adults learn to work together. They brighten meetings with humor while driving home important points.

But only if your performers can act.

If your children's ministry is like most—that is, if your children aren't all movie stars and your volunteers aren't all Tony award winners—your experience with skits may be nothing to write home about. If your group is "theatrically challenged," you may find you're avoiding skits or relying entirely on canned, prerecorded puppet shows.

Your dilemma: Should you keep less-skilled kids and helpers off the stage, and make them feel left out? Or should you use everyone and limp through some ineffective and embarrassing efforts?

Fortunately, there's a third choice. It's *Instant Skits for Children's Ministry!*

Real Fun, Real Truths—for Real Children

What do you want in a skit? It's all here—from pratfalls to movie parodies. Want solid, Bible-based messages? They're here, too—covering important topics, such as forgiveness, entertainment choices, and being a Christian at school.

You'll get more than fun and truthful messages with *Instant Skits for Children's Ministry*, though. You get *help* with making each skit *work*.

Every script in this book has been prepared with *real* kids and helpers in mind. Instead of long speeches and big words, you'll find easy-to-read dialogue that helps kids play parts, too. And to give you maximum flexibility, each skit can be performed by live actors, puppets, or a combination of both.

Best of all, *Instant Skits for Children's Ministry* shows your actors and puppeteers how to draw the best possible reading—and the most meaning—from every line. Each script features simple facial-expression symbols to instantly show kids and adults how to put the right feeling into each line. We've also printed the words that should be emphasized in capital letters to beat the "monotone syndrome" and ensure that everyone catches key concepts.

The result? Skits that build confidence. Skits that let you cast almost anyone. Skits that cut mistakes to a minimum so the message can't miss. Skits that every child in the audience can understand—and remember.

Use *Instant Skits for Children's Ministry* in any of your children's programs—Sunday school, children's church, club meetings, vacation Bible school—whenever you want to make your point in a fresh, funny, memorable way. With each script you'll find Bible verses to read, related topics to explore, easy setup ideas, puppet options, discussion questions, and extra touches you might choose to add. You'll find so much, in fact, that you can turn each skit into a complete meeting of its own—if you want to.

And After the Skit?

Children's ministry doesn't end when the skit's over, so the skits in this book don't end there either. You can take advantage of the discussion questions provided in the To Talk About section to help your kids fully grasp and apply important truths addressed in the skits.

As you lead children in post-play pondering, remember that variety and interaction help to make discussion exciting. Use large groups, small groups, pairs, and trios. Try writing questions on table tennis balls and tossing them into the group. Have kids act out their answers as if they were playing Charades. The possibilities are endless!

A great skit can be one of your sharpest tools—if it works. Here's your chance to get more of that power off the page and into the hearts of your children where it belongs.

Key to Expression Symbols

To help actors know at a glance how to say their lines, the dialogue in this book includes simple facial-expression symbols. Most performers will quickly grasp the emotions represented by the symbols, so you shouldn't need to explain them. For *your* reference, though, here are the *official* meanings of the little faces.

Calm, Pleasant

Happy, Hopeful

Laughing

Relieved

Serious, Earnest

Smug, Boastful, Condescending

Shy, Innocent

Nervous, Worried

Scared

Surprised, Shocked

Screaming, Hysterical

Malicious, Sneaky

Disgusted

Irritated, Complaining

Sad, Depressed, Sorry

Puzzled, Unsure, Thinking

Sarcastic, Skeptical

Mumbling, Whispering

Bored, Disinterested

Slick, Phony

Sheepish, Embarrassed

Proud, Haughty

Crying

Excited

Sick, Disoriented, Tired

Emotionless

Crazy, Goofy

Angry

Pained, Strained

Hypnotized, Zombielike

The Book of Joe

Topic: Why Bad Things Happen

Scriptures You Might Read: Genesis 3:17-19; Job 2:7-10

The Scene: A playground

The Simple Setup: No set is required. All actors may wear casual clothes; Friend 2 should wear a watch. Actors of either gender could play all roles with minor word changes. (Note: Be sure your actors know that the name of the biblical character, Job, is pronounced "jobe"—like robe—not "job.")

Puppet Options: You could use puppets for all the roles. Or, if you want to mix puppets and live actors, cast a child as **Joe**.

Extra Touches: To increase **Joe's** visibility while he's lying down, have him drape himself over a "boulder" made of blanket-covered cardboard boxes.

The Characters:
> **Joe**, who's in distress
> **Friend 1**, a would-be comforter
> **Friend 2**, another would-be comforter
> **Friend 3**, still another you-know-what

*(As the skit begins, **Joe** is lying at center stage, moaning.)*

Joe: OHH…OHH…WOE is ME. WOE is ME.

*(**Friends 1, 2,** and **3** enter.)*

Friend 1: Hey, LOOK! It's JOE!

Friend 2: Joe, what happened to YOU?

Friend 3: You look AWFUL!

Joe: OH, WOE is ME.

Friend 1: Boy, he must REALLY be HURTING!

Friend 2: Let's stay here and COMFORT him.

Friend 3: How can we HELP you, Joe?

Joe: OH, WOE is ME.

Friend 1: You know, this REMINDS me of something.

Friend 2: YEAH, a person is on the GROUND, suffering TERRIBLY, and his FRIENDS come by to COMFORT him…

Friend 3: RIGHT! It's just like a story in the BIBLE!

Friend 1: DAVID and GOLIATH!

Friend 2: DANIEL in the den of LIONS!

Friend 3: NO! It's like the book of JOB!

Friend 1: Of COURSE! The book of JOB. *(Pauses.)* What's the book of JOB?

Friend 3: It's about this guy who always OBEYS GOD, but he has to SUFFER. He loses his CHILDREN, his MONEY, his SERVANTS, EVERYTHING. He ends up sitting on the GROUND, covered with SORES.

Friend 2: YUCK!

Friend 3: Then his FRIENDS come by to visit.

Friend 1: That's US!

Friend 3: And they try to figure out WHY Job is SUFFERING.

Joe: OH, WOE is ME.

Friend 2: SO WHY do you think Joe is SUFFERING?

Friend 1: Well, it's CLEAR, isn't it? I mean, he MUST have done something WRONG. And now he's being PUNISHED.

Friend 2: What do you think he DID?

Friend 1: Well, he's in pretty bad SHAPE, so it must have been a really BAD SIN. Maybe he ROBBED a BANK.

Friend 3: ROBBED a BANK? Our friend JOE?

Joe: OH, WOE is ME.

Friend 1: No, I take that BACK. He's SO UNHAPPY; he must have KILLED SOMEBODY. Or maybe he SAT IN THE BACK ROW AT CHURCH and BLEW BUBBLES WITH HIS GUM.

Friend 2: No WAY! You've got this all WRONG. Joe isn't suffering because he's being PUNISHED. He's suffering because God is trying to TEACH him something.

Friend 3: Like WHAT?

Friend 2: Um...that he should PRAY more. Or maybe that he ought to become a MISSIONARY when he grows up.

Joe: OHHH...

Friend 1: Hold ON. If God wants to TEACH Joe something, why doesn't God just TEACH him something? When MRS. APPLE at SCHOOL wants us to LEARN something, she doesn't make us SUFFER.

Friend 3: She does TOO!

Friend 1: YOU know what I mean! She doesn't make us ROLL AROUND ON THE GROUND and try to GUESS what the lesson is. GOD has to be at LEAST as good a teacher as MRS. APPLE, RIGHT?

Friend 2: Well...

Friend 3: Sorry, but you're BOTH mixed up about this whole SUFFERING thing. Joe isn't suffering because he did something WRONG. And he isn't SUFFERING because God is trying to TEACH him something.

Friend 1: So WHY is he SUFFERING?

Friend 3: Because the DEVIL is ATTACKING him. Joe must have been doing something RIGHT, not something WRONG. And THAT made the devil so MAD that he made Joe SICK or HURT or...uh...Say, JOE, what IS the matter with you, ANYWAY?

Joe: OHHH...I...I was trying to OPEN a CAN OF POP, and I...I CHIPPED my FINGERNAIL.

Friend 1: You CHIPPED YOUR FINGERNAIL?

Friend 2: WHAT?

Friend 3: I thought it was something BAD!

Friend 1: Here you ARE, LYING on the GROUND and MOANING, and all you did was CHIP YOUR FINGERNAIL?

Joe: *(Sitting up)* WELL...YEAH.

Friend 2: And we wasted all that time COMFORTING you?

Friend 3: And trying to figure out why you were SUFFERING?

Joe: *(Standing)* UH...YEAH.

Friend 1: I'll show YOU suffering, you PHONY!

Joe: *(Running away)* OHHH...WOE is ME!

*(**Friend 1** chases **Joe** offstage; both exit the stage.)*

Friend 2: *(Checking watch)* Oh, NO! We spent so much time trying to help JOE that we missed the start of the GAME we were going to! Oh, WHY did this AWFUL DISASTER have to happen? WHY?

Friend 3: *(Patting **Friend 2** on the back as they both exit the stage)* I don't know, friend. I JUST DON'T KNOW.

● **To Talk About:**
- Which of Joe's friends made the most sense to you? Why?
- Do different people suffer for different reasons? Explain.
- Read Genesis 3:17-19. How does this help to explain suffering?
- How could you be really helpful in the following situations?
  - a friend's parents are getting divorced
  - a friend is recovering from a serious car accident
  - a friend has lost a brother or sister in a war
  - a friend's house has burned down

● **Other Topical Tie-Ins:**

Friendship   Helping others   Facing trouble

Cliff's Notes

Topic: Cheating

Scriptures You Might Read: Leviticus 6:1-5; Proverbs 10:9

The Scene: A living room

The Simple Setup: Place two chairs at center stage with a small table nearby. Put a fine-line, washable-ink pen on the table. You'll also need a history textbook (a real one or a book with a homemade cover that reads, "U.S. History"). All actors may wear casual clothes. Pretest the pen to make sure the ink really washes off—or just have **Cliff** pretend to write on himself. If **Cliff** does pretend to write on himself, he should wear long sleeves and pants to cover the supposedly written-on areas of his body. (Note: Before the performance, you might want to help **Claire** with the pronunciation of some of the names in this skit.)

Puppet Options: You could use puppets for all the roles, though it might be a challenge for the puppet **Cliff** to write on himself. In that case, or if you want to mix puppets and live actors, cast a child or leader as **Cliff**.

Extra Touches: If you'd like, include more living room furniture to help identify the setting.

The Characters:
> **Cliff**, a boy who hates to study
> **Claire**, a good student
> **Mom**, Claire's mother

(*As the skit begins,* **Cliff** *and* **Claire** *are sitting on the chairs.* **Claire** *has the history textbook in her hands.* **Mom** *is standing near the stage exit.*)

Mom: ALL right, you two, have a good time STUDYING.

Claire: THANKS, Mom.

(**Mom** *exits the stage.*)

Cliff: Have a GOOD TIME studying? Is your mom CRAZY?

Claire: Not that I KNOW of. But this HISTORY TEST TOMORROW shouldn't be TOO bad, Cliff. All we have to do is LEARN THE ANSWERS.

Cliff: LEARN? I've never learned ANYTHING in school! Except my BUS NUMBER—EIGHT and a HALF. No, WAIT. That's my SHOE SIZE.

Claire: If you haven't learned ANYTHING in school, how come you keep PASSING TESTS?

Cliff: I have a little SECRET. *(Looks around to make sure no one is listening.)* I WRITE the ANSWERS on my ARM.

Claire: YOU WRITE THE ANSWERS ON YOUR ARM?

Cliff: SHH! It's a SECRET!

Claire: But...

Cliff: *(Interrupting)* Now WHERE'S a PEN? *(Spots the pen and picks it up.)* AH! HERE'S one!

Claire: But you SHOULDN'T...

Cliff: *(Interrupting)* I know, I KNOW. You think it's CHEATING. But EVERYBODY does it.

Claire: That's not TRUE!

Cliff: BESIDES, it doesn't HURT anybody. I write the answers on my ARM, I get a GOOD GRADE, and everybody is HAPPY—my PARENTS, the TEACHER, ME. ESPECIALLY me.

Claire: Cliff, I wouldn't DO that if I were you.

Cliff: I'm sure you WOULDN'T! But MY way is FASTER than LEARNING. So YOU get ready for the test YOUR way, and I'll get ready in MY way. We'll SEE who gets done FIRST.

Claire: *(Sighing)* OK.

Cliff: On your MARK, get SET, GO!

Claire: *(Looking at book)* The AMERICAN REVOLUTIONARY WAR began in 1775. Hmm, 1775—got to REMEMBER that.

Cliff: *(Writing on his arm)* AMERICAN REVOLUTION...1775.

Claire: *(Faster, turning pages in book)* ELI WHITNEY invented the COTTON GIN in 1793. The LOUISIANA PURCHASE was in 1803.

Cliff: *(Writing faster on his arm)* Eli WHITNEY, Louisiana PURCHASE.

Claire: *(Faster, turning pages in book)* ABRAHAM LINCOLN became PRESIDENT in 1861. GEORGE WASHINGTON CARVER was born in 1864. The CIVIL WAR began in 1861.

Cliff: *(Writing faster on his arm)* Hey, WAIT! I'm running out of ROOM! Got to switch to the OTHER arm! *(Begins writing on other arm)* George Washington CARVER, Civil WAR.

Claire: *(Faster, turning pages in book)* ALEXANDER GRAHAM BELL patented the TELEPHONE in 1876. The SPANISH-AMERICAN WAR was in 1898. THEODORE ROOSEVELT became president in 1901. HENRY FORD began selling the MODEL T car in 1908. WORLD WAR I started in 1914.

Cliff: HOLD it! I'm running out of ROOM again! I'll have to write on my LEG. *(Begins writing on leg.)*

Claire: *(Faster, turning pages in book)* The GREAT DEPRESSION began in 1929. WORLD WAR II ended in 1945. The KOREAN WAR began in 1950. MARTIN LUTHER KING, JR. spoke at the March on WASHINGTON in 1963. PRESIDENT KENNEDY was assassinated in 1963.

Cliff: OTHER leg! *(Begins writing on other leg.)*

Claire: *(Faster, turning pages in book)* The first men walked on the MOON in 1969. PRESIDENT NIXON resigned in 1974. The VIETNAM WAR ended in 1975.

Cliff: I'll...I'll write on my STOMACH! *(Lifts his shirt a little and begins scribbling.)*

Claire: *(Faster, turning pages in book)* The United States celebrated its TWO HUNDREDTH BIRTHDAY in 1976. The CHALLENGER SPACE SHUTTLE blew up in 1986. The BERLIN WALL was torn down in 1989. The PERSIAN GULF WAR was fought in 1991. BILL CLINTON was impeached in 1998.

Cliff: *(Pauses, panting from all the scribbling.)* Is that IT?

Claire: YEP.

Cliff: I WIN! I've got ALL THE ANSWERS on me! All I have to do is PEEK at them, but YOU still have to LEARN all of them. That'll take you ALL NIGHT.

Claire: I guess you're RIGHT, Cliff. You WIN.

Cliff: You thought I couldn't DO it, huh? YOU thought I'd RUN OUT OF ROOM! Boy, did I...

Mom: *(Enters the stage, interrupting)* EXCUSE me. Has anyone seen my LAUNDRY MARKER?

Cliff: LAUNDRY marker?

Mom: YES. It's a SPECIAL MARKER with ink that never, EVER comes off. *(Spots the pen in **Cliff's** hand.)* Oh, THERE it is. THANK you, Cliff. *(Takes the pen and exits the stage.)*

Cliff: SPECIAL MARKER? Ink that NEVER COMES OFF?

Claire: Well, maybe with SANDPAPER.

Cliff: SANDPAPER? I'll have to SANDPAPER my ENTIRE BODY! OH NO! *(Runs off the stage.)*

Claire: HUH, THAT might take him... ALL NIGHT! *(Smiles and exits the stage with the book.)*

● **To Talk About:**

- Is cheating a shortcut to learning or just to better grades? What's the difference?
- Do you think it's true that cheaters never prosper? Why or why not?
- Would you like to have Jesus as a study partner? Why or why not?
- Which of the following do you think would be the surest way to get kids to stop cheating, and why do you think so?
  - watch them with TV cameras as they take tests
  - pay them to be honest
  - help them to become followers of Jesus
  - give them more study time

● **Other Topical Tie-Ins:**

School stress   Honesty   Peer pressure

Clueless

Topic: God's Creation

Scriptures You Might Read: Genesis 1; Romans 1:18-20

The Scene: Nineteenth-century London

The Simple Setup: No set or props are required. An offstage helper can provide the knocking sound. British accents would be a nice touch if your performers can speak in an accent; if not, have them stick with their regular dialects. (Note: Before the performance, you might want to explain to **Holmes** the meaning of the phrases, "the game's afoot" and "elementary, my dear Flopson.")

Puppet Options: You could use puppets for all the roles. Any adult-looking male puppets would do for the two detectives, especially if you can add old-fashioned hats and coats. If you want to mix puppets and live actors, give one of your leaders or children a cameo role as **Lady**.

Extra Touches: You might have **Holmes** wear a deerstalker cap and raincoat and carry a bubble pipe and large magnifying glass. **Flopson** could wear a bowler hat and suit.

The Characters:
    Shirtbox Holmes, a dense detective
    Doctor Flopson, his dimwitted assistant
    Lady, damsel in distress

*(As the skit begins, **Doctor Flopson** enters the stage.)*

Flopson:		*(Speaking to the audience)* It was a DARK and STORMY NIGHT. Really it was rather RAINY—but not exactly what you would call a STORM. Or maybe it was SNOWING. And SUNNY. Except that, if it was NIGHT, it couldn't be SUNNY, COULD it? So maybe it was during the DAY. Yes, THAT'S it. There was a TORNADO, I think, and just a BIT of a TIDAL WAVE…
Holmes:		*(Entering the stage, interrupting)* DOCTOR FLOPSON!
Flopson:		Uh, YES, Holmes?
Holmes:		What are you DOING?
Flopson:		Um, I was just telling everyone about our latest ADVENTURE.

Holmes: It SOUNDED like you were giving the WEATHER REPORT.

Flopson: Oh. Yes. Quite SO.

Holmes: Just get on with the STORY, WON'T you?

Flopson: Of COURSE, Holmes. *(Speaking to the audience)* Uh, BACK to our latest ADVENTURE. I call it "The STRANGE CASE of the MYSTERIOUSLY MISSING MAKER of the ENTIRE UNIVERSE AND EVERYTHING."

Holmes: Doctor FLOPSON!

Flopson: Uh, YES, Holmes?

Holmes: That's too LONG. Just call it "The CASE of the MISSING MAKER."

Flopson: Oh, JOLLY GOOD, Holmes! *(Speaking to the audience)* You can see why SHIRTBOX HOLMES is known as the WORLD'S SMARTEST DETECTIVE. And why I, DOCTOR FLOPSON, am only his HUMBLE HELPER.

Holmes: Yes, we can ALL see that. Now on with the STORY.

Flopson: As you WISH, Holmes. It all began as Holmes and I were sitting in his place on BAKERY STREET. We were drinking TEA and eating TRUMPETS...

Holmes: *(Interrupting)* CRUMPETS! We were eating CRUMPETS! You can't eat TRUMPETS! TRUMPETS are MUSICAL INSTRUMENTS made of METAL!

Flopson: Oh. Well. Suddenly there was a KNOCK at the DOOR.

(Offstage helper knocks.)

Flopson: In came a LADY, looking VERY upset.

Lady: *(Entering the stage)* EXCUSE me. SHIRTBOX HOLMES, WORLD'S SMARTEST DETECTIVE? I've come because...

Holmes: *(Interrupting)* No, don't TELL me! *(Pauses.)* For YEARS, you have been BOTHERED by a BURNING QUESTION.

Lady: Why, that's RIGHT!

Holmes: You need the ANSWER to one of life's GREATEST MYSTERIES.

Lady: Yes...YES...

Holmes: You want to know...WHO MADE THE UNIVERSE!

Lady: EXACTLY! Oh, Mr. HOLMES! You ARE the WORLD'S SMARTEST DETECTIVE!

Holmes: YES, I KNOW. You may COUNT on us, madam. We will find out WHO MADE THE UNIVERSE.

Lady: Oh, THANK you, Mr. Holmes! *(Exits the stage.)*

Holmes: COME, Doctor Flopson! The GAME'S AFOOT! *(Exits the stage.)*

Flopson: *(Speaking to the audience)* And so I followed the great SHIRTBOX HOLMES as he tried to solve the MYSTERY of who made the universe. Our FIRST stop—the ZOO.

*(**Holmes** enters the stage.)*

Flopson: I SAY, Holmes, why are we at the ZOO?

Holmes: ELEMENTARY, my dear FLOPSON! We're here to see all the AMAZING ANIMALS! Did you know there are almost TEN THOUSAND kinds of BIRDS? And more than TWENTY-FIVE THOUSAND kinds of animals that are like LOBSTERS and CRABS?

Flopson: That IS amazing, Holmes!

Holmes: Guess how many kinds of INSECTS there are, Flopson.

Flopson: Uh, TWO?

Holmes: No, there are almost ONE MILLION!

Flopson: My GOODNESS, Holmes! WHO could have made SO MANY different kinds of ANIMALS?

Holmes: I don't KNOW yet, Flopson. Let's keep LOOKING! *(Exits the stage.)*

Flopson: *(Speaking to the audience)* And so I KEPT following the great Shirtbox Holmes as he tried to figure out WHO MADE THE UNIVERSE. NEXT stop: OUTER SPACE!

*(**Holmes** enters the stage.)*

Flopson: I SAY, Holmes, what are we doing in OUTER SPACE? It's a bit hard to

BREATHE, I must SAY.

Holmes: Oh, STOP COMPLAINING, Flopson. Look at these amazing PLANETS! Did you know that the EARTH is ninety-five million miles from the SUN, so it's the ONLY planet known to support LIFE?

Flopson: INCREDIBLE, Holmes!

Holmes: Now, WHO could have known EXACTLY how far the EARTH needed to be from the SUN? And WHO could have been POWERFUL enough to PUT it there?

Flopson: It wasn't ME, Holmes.

Holmes: I KNOW that, Flopson. What I DON'T know yet is WHO MADE THE UNIVERSE. Let's keep LOOKING. *(Exits the stage.)*

Flopson: *(Speaking to the audience)* Once more I followed the great Shirtbox Holmes as he tried to solve the mystery of WHO MADE THE UNIVERSE. Our FINAL stop: Holmes' place on BAKERY STREET.

*(**Holmes** enters the stage.)*

Flopson: I SAY, Holmes, there's nothing amazing HERE.

Holmes: Ah, but there IS, Flopson. I'm talking about…the HUMAN BODY.

Flopson: The HUMAN BODY? What's so amazing about THAT?

Holmes: Surely YOU know, Flopson. After all, you're a DOCTOR.

Flopson: I'M not a DOCTOR, Holmes. "DOCTOR" is just my FIRST NAME.

Holmes: WHAT?

Flopson: I'm MUCH too DUMB to be a REAL doctor.

Holmes: I knew that. But did YOU know that your HEART pumps about THREE HUNDRED QUARTS of BLOOD every HOUR, which is more than SIX HUNDRED THOUSAND GALLONS each YEAR?

Flopson: I had NO IDEA!

Holmes: And in a usual LIFETIME, your heart will pump more than FORTY-SIX MILLION gallons of blood.

Flopson: SMASHING! But WHO could have created a HUMAN HEART, Holmes?

Holmes: ELEMENTARY, my dear Flopson. The answer is…NO ONE!

Flopson: NO one?

Holmes: I've SOLVED the MYSTERY, Flopson. WHO made the ANIMALS, the PLANETS, our amazing BODIES? NO ONE!

Flopson: But Holmes…

Holmes: Don't you SEE, Flopson? I couldn't create these amazing things. So if SOMEONE created these amazing things, that person would be SMARTER than I am. And THAT is…IMPOSSIBLE.

Flopson: Because YOU are the world's SMARTEST detective!

Holmes: RIGHT.

Flopson: HOLMES, you're a GENIUS. Let's go tell that LADY you've SOLVED the MYSTERY.

Holmes: I'm OFF, Flopson! The GAME'S AFOOT! *(Exits the stage.)*

Flopson: *(Speaking to the audience)* And THAT is the story of how the great SHIRTBOX HOLMES discovered that NOBODY made the universe. What an AMAZING CASE, especially because…we didn't have a CLUE! *(Exits the stage.)*

● **To Talk About:**

- What clues did the detectives have, if they'd just paid attention? What clues about the Maker of the universe have you discovered?
- Other than God making the universe, how do people explain the beginning of everything? Which explanations make the most sense to you? Why?
- Which is most amazing to you: the animal kingdom, outer space, or the human body? Why?
- If one person believes no one made the universe and a second person believes God made it, how might each person react in the following situations?
  - walking on the moon
  - hearing that a friend is very sick
  - deciding whether to throw litter into a river

● **Other Topical Tie-Ins:**

God's existence   Faith   Science and the Bible

The Collection

Topic: Giving

Scriptures You Might Read: Luke 6:38; 21:1-4

The Scene: A church pew

The Simple Setup: Set three chairs in a row to suggest a church pew. You'll also need two cardboard boxes, a sports card, a beanbag, a penny, and a collection plate. The actors should dress as people typically dress in your church. Actors of either gender could play all roles, with minor word changes. (Note: Before the performance, you might want to help the actors with the pronunciation of some of the proper nouns in this skit.)

Puppet Options: You could use puppets for all the roles. If you choose to use puppets, you won't need chairs or cardboard boxes. Simply have puppets for **Kid 1** and **Kid 2** get their props from under the puppet stage. If you'd like to include a live actor, cast a child or leader as **Usher**.

Extra Touches: If you'd like, use a real church pew instead of chairs.

The Characters:

    Kid 1, a proud collector of sports cards
    Kid 2, a haughty collector of beanie baggies
    Kid 3, a humble collector of pennies
    Usher, a polite and friendly church usher

*(As the skit begins, **Kids 1, 2,** and **3** enter and sit on the "church pew" chairs. **Kid 1** is holding a large cardboard box on his or her lap, as is **Kid 2**.)*

Kid 1: *(Speaking to **Kid 2**)* PSST! HEY! Did you hear what the PASTOR just said?

Kid 2: Of COURSE I did! He said it's time to TAKE UP THE COLLECTION.

Kid 1: And did you BRING your COLLECTION?

Kid 2: Of COURSE! I ALWAYS bring my COLLECTION for when they TAKE UP THE COLLECTION.

Kid 1: As USUAL, I brought my collection of SPORTS CARDS.

Kid 2: And as USUAL, I brought my collection of BEANIE BAGGIES.

Kid 1: (Pointing at **Kid 3**) What did HE bring?

Kid 2: Looks like he didn't bring ANYTHING.

Kid 1: HMPH! Doesn't he know you're supposed to BRING YOUR COLLECTION for when they TAKE UP THE COLLECTION?

Kid 2: The NERVE of some people!

Kid 1: (Speaking to **Kid 3**) EXCUSE me!

Kid 3: Who, ME?

Kid 1: Yes, YOU! Didn't anyone TELL you you're supposed to BRING YOUR COLLECTION for when they TAKE UP THE COLLECTION?

Kid 3: Um...YES.

Kid 2: Well, what kind of collection IS it?

Kid 3: A PENNY collection.

Kid 1: (Speaking to **Kid 2**) A PENNY collection?

(**Kids 1** and **2** snicker.)

Kid 2: And where IS this penny collection?

Kid 3: (Holding up a penny) Right HERE.

Kid 1: That's IT?

Kid 2: You call that a COLLECTION?

(**Kids 1** and **2** snicker.)

Kid 3: It's...all I HAVE.

Kid 1: (Speaking to **Kid 2**) Talk about PATHETIC!

Kid 2: (Speaking to **Kid 1**) Who let him IN here, anyway?

Kid 3: Oh, LOOK! Here comes the COLLECTION PLATE.

Kid 1: At LAST!

Kid 2: This is my FAVORITE PART of church, you know—the part where EVERYONE gets to see how GIVING I am.

Kid 1: Same HERE. *(Looking into the cardboard box)* Let's SEE. Which card from my collection should I put in the PLATE? So many to CHOOSE from: BASEBALL...HOCKEY...FOOTBALL...HACKEY-SACK...

Kid 2: *(Pointing into Kid 1's box)* Say, THERE'S a nice one. Why don't you put THAT in the collection plate?

Kid 1: Are you KIDDING? That's a MARK MCGWIRE baseball card! He set a record for HOME RUNS. It's going to be worth MONEY someday.

Kid 2: Oh. *(Pointing into Kid 1's box)* Well, how about THAT one?

Kid 1: No WAY! That's a BUBBA BALLOONY basketball card!

Kid 2: BUBBA BALLOONY? Who's THAT?

Kid 1: He's the THIRD COUSIN of the NEIGHBOR of the UNCLE of the DENTIST of MICHAEL JORDAN! THIS card is going to be worth MONEY someday! *(Pauses.)* Well, maybe a LITTLE money.

Kid 2: Then what are you going to put in the COLLECTION PLATE?

Kid 1: *(Pulls a card from the box and holds it up.)* THIS. It's a HUGO MCDORGLE card.

Kid 2: Never HEARD of him.

Kid 1: Of COURSE not! He's a PING-PONG player. He's LOST EVERY GAME he's ever PLAYED, including one he played ALL BY HIMSELF. It'll NEVER be worth much.

Kid 2: Good THINKING!

Kid 1: *(Speaking to Kid 2)* So what are YOU going to put in the collection plate?

Kid 2: Why, something from my BEANIE BAGGIE COLLECTION, of course.

Kid 1:   *(Pointing into **Kid 2**'s box)* How about that WHITE one with the LONG TAIL?

Kid 2:   NO! That's TOMMY THE TAPEWORM! He's RARE! They made only THREE of him, and now he's RETIRED. He's in MINT CONDITION. And he has his TAG. And...

Kid 1:   *(Interrupting)* OK, I get the IDEA. *(Pointing into **Kid 2**'s box)* What about this GREEN one with all the LEGS?

Kid 2:   Not on your LIFE! That's SYLVESTER THE SLIME BEETLE! TRUE, they made more than SEVEN MILLION of him, and my DOG chewed off his HEAD. But I think he's kind of CUTE.

Kid 1:   Then what are you going to put in the COLLECTION PLATE?

Kid 2:   *(Takes a plain beanbag from the box and holds it up)* THIS! It's BORIS THE BACTERIA! They made a BILLION of them and couldn't GIVE them away. BESIDES, my DAD ran OVER it with his CAR.

Kid 1:   A PERFECT CHOICE!

*(**Usher** enters the stage with a collection plate.)*

Kid 2:   WELL, it's about TIME you got here.

*(**Usher** hands **Kid 1** the collection plate.)*

Kid 1:   *(Taking the collection plate)* Here we GO, everyone! See how GIVING I am? I'm giving one of the DEAR CARDS from my COLLECTION. *(Drops card onto the plate, then passes the plate to **Kid 2**.)*

Kid 2:   *(Taking the collection plate)* LOOK, everybody! Isn't this AMAZING? I'm putting one of my FAVORITE BEANIE BAGGIES in the COLLECTION PLATE. *(Drops beanbag onto the plate, then passes the plate to **Kid 3**.)*

Kid 1:   *(Speaking to **Kid 2**)* OOH! What's HE going to give?

Kid 2:   *(Speaking to **Kid 1**)* Yeah, he's only got ONE PENNY in his whole COLLECTION!

*(**Kids 1** and **2** snicker.)*

Kid 3:   *(Looking up as if to heaven)* LORD, I...I'm SORRY my COLLECTION is so SMALL. This ONE PENNY is all I HAVE, but YOU can have it now. *(Places the penny on the plate, then gives the plate to **Usher**.)*

Kid 1: *(Speaking to **Kid 2**)* Totally EMBARRASSING!

Kid 2: *(Speaking to **Kid 1**)* Why did he have to sit next to US?

Usher: *(Takes the penny from the plate and looks at it.)* WOW! This is a RARE PENNY—A 1919S with LINCOLN'S HEAD UPSIDE DOWN! It's worth at least FIVE HUNDRED DOLLARS! The CHURCH can SELL this penny and buy ALL KINDS OF THINGS we NEED! *(Speaking to **Kid 3**)* THANK you!

Kid 3: You're WELCOME!

Kid 2: HEY, what about US? WE gave stuff too!

Usher: YOU TWO gave a LITTLE from your collections. But *(indicating **Kid 3**)* HE gave everything he HAD.  *(Speaking to **Kid 3**)* HEY, come with ME. You can help me count the MONEY.

Kid 1: What a SHOWOFF!

Kid 2: I HATE it when that happens!

*(**Kids 1** and **2** get up and start to leave.)*

Kid 1: SO what will you bring NEXT week? Your BELLYBUTTON LINT COLLECTION?

Kid 2: Are you KIDDING? There's some REALLY VALUABLE LINT in there! There's the PURPLE lint I got when I wore a GRAPE COSTUME in the SCHOOL PLAY and the WHITE lint I got when I wore DIAPERS...

*(**Kid 1** and **2** exit the stage.)*

● **To Talk About:**

- What does it really mean to "take up the collection" in church? If this is done in your church, how do you feel when it happens?
- Which of your possessions would be the most difficult for you to put in the collection plate because of its value to you? Why?
- How is this skit like Jesus' story in Luke 21:1-4? What do you think Jesus wanted people to learn from that story?
- What do you think Jesus would like you to put in the collection plate next time it comes around?

● **Other Topical Tie-Ins:**

Material things   Giving God your best   Making the most of what God gives you

Comfort and Joy

Topic: Christmas

Scriptures You Might Read: Matthew 8:20; Luke 2:1-7

The Scene: A room at church

The Simple Setup: You'll need a table with three chairs around it. **Kid 1** should have a pencil and a few sheets of paper. All actors may wear casual clothes. Actors of either gender could play all roles, with minor word changes.

Puppet Options: You could use puppets for all the roles. If you'd like to mix puppets and actors, cast a leader as **Teacher**.

Extra Touches: If you'd like to more clearly identify the setting as a room at church, decorate the wall with a bulletin board, Bible verse poster, or other appropriate item.

The Characters:
> **Teacher,** a friendly but serious adult
> **Kid 1,** who's trying to do the right thing
> **Kid 2,** who's totally self-centered

(As the skit begins, all the characters are seated at the table.)

Teacher: *(Speaking to **Kids 1** and **2**)* I want to THANK you for agreeing to plan this year's LIVING NATIVITY SCENE for the FRONT LAWN of the CHURCH. I KNOW you'll do a GREAT job. Now, I have some WORK to do next DOOR. YOU start PLANNING, and I'll be back in a few MINUTES. *(Exits the stage.)*

Kid 1: OK, any IDEAS for the LIVING NATIVITY SCENE?

Kid 2: Well, for ONE thing, we have to get rid of the SHEEP.

Kid 1: WHY?

Kid 2: Five letters: S...M...E...L...L.

Kid 1: SMELL?

Kid 2:   Good WORK, SMARTY.

Kid 1:   But you can't have a LIVING NATIVITY SCENE without ANIMALS.

Kid 2:   OK, you can use a HAMSTER.

Kid 1:   A HAMSTER?

Kid 2:   Or a DUCK. Take your PICK.

Kid 1:   (Sighing and writing) "One HAMSTER."

Kid 2:   And LOSE those grubby-looking SHEPHERDS. You don't need SHEPHERDS for a HAMSTER, anyway.

Kid 1:   (Writing) "No SHEPHERDS."

Kid 2:   And we won't need any STRAW, of course. It makes me SNEEZE.

Kid 1:   (Writing) "No STRAW."

Kid 2:   And while we're AT it, let's DROP that STABLE.

Kid 1:   DROP the STABLE? But wasn't JESUS born in a...

Kid 2:   (Interrupting) It's way too DRAFTY. I could catch a COLD.

Kid 1:   What kind of building do you WANT?

Kid 2:   A cozy little COTTAGE would be fine. As long as it has a good HEATER.

Kid 1:   (Writing) "COTTAGE with HEATER."

Kid 2:   And a MICROWAVE OVEN.

Kid 1:   A MICROWAVE OVEN?

Kid 2:   For SNACKS. I'll get HUNGRY standing out there, you know.

Kid 1:   (Writing) "One MICROWAVE OVEN."

Kid 2:   Yeah, I guess ONE is enough. But we'll probably need TWO TVs.

Kid 1: TWO TVs?

Kid 2: Of COURSE. One will be hooked up to the VCR so we can watch MOVIES. The OTHER will be for VIDEO GAMES. You don't want us to get BORED, do you?

Kid 1: But—a LIVING NATIVITY SCENE with two TVs?

Kid 2: You're RIGHT. We'll need THREE.

Kid 1: WHAT?

Kid 2: In case one of us wants to watch a CHRISTMAS SPECIAL—maybe FROSTY THE SNOWMAN.

Kid 1: *(Sighing and writing)* "Three TVs."

Kid 2: NOW, about the FURNITURE.

Kid 1: RIGHT. *(Writing)* "One wooden MANGER."

Kid 2: MANGER? I don't mean for the BABY. I mean for US!

Kid 1: But on the FIRST Christmas they didn't have...

Kid 2: *(Interrupting)* We'll need a ROCKING CHAIR for MARY. A nice RECLINER for JOSEPH. And a big comfy SOFA for the TWELVE WISE MEN.

Kid 1: TWELVE wise men?

Kid 2: We'll need at least TWELVE to CARRY ALL OUR PRESENTS! And none of those WEIRD presents, EITHER. Who wants FRANKENSTEIN and MYRRH, or WHATEVER those are? I want stuff like CDs and GIFT CERTIFICATES.

Kid 1: But the presents aren't for US.

Kid 2: Of COURSE they are! Do you think I'm going to sit out there in a BATHROBE for NOTHING?

Kid 1: *(Writing)* "Comfy furniture. TWELVE wise men with CDs."

*(**Teacher** enters the stage.)*

Teacher: SO how are we DOING? What's our LIVING NATIVITY SCENE going to LOOK like?

Kid 1: *(Handing notes to **Teacher**)* Like THIS.

Teacher: *(Reading)* "One HAMSTER, no SHEPHERDS, no STRAW, COTTAGE with HEATER, one MICROWAVE OVEN, three TVs, comfy FURNITURE, twelve WISE MEN with CDs?" But THIS isn't what I had in mind at ALL!

Kid 2: YEAH, but...

Teacher: *(Interrupting)* I'm afraid we're out of TIME for this meeting. You can meet NEXT week to plan something a bit more...REAL. I'll see you THEN. *(Exits the stage.)*

Kid 2: REAL? I don't want to be in a REAL nativity scene. The REAL first Christmas was UNCOMFORTABLE! It was YUCKY! It was...GROSS! *(Pauses.)* Sorry, but I QUIT! *(Exits the stage.)*

Kid 1: Well, everyone KNOWS it just wouldn't be CHRISTMAS without REAL animals and REAL straw. *(Writing notes while starting to exit)* "One SLEIGH full of TOYS, EIGHT tiny REINDEER..." *(Exits the stage.)*

● To Talk About:

- What was "uncomfortable," "yucky," and "gross" about the first Christmas?
- Who is Christmas *for*? Why?
- Have you ever been in a living Nativity or Christmas play? Did it help you think about the real meaning of Christmas? Why or why not?
- Which of the following would help you think more about Jesus this Christmas?
  - getting fewer presents
  - giving more presents
  - putting only angels and stars on the Christmas tree
  - spending more time at church
  - something else

● Other Topical Tie-Ins:

Humility   What Jesus is like   Materialism

The Coverup

Topic: Being a Christian at School

Scriptures You Might Read: 1 Peter 3:13-17; 4:14-16

The Scene: A hallway at school

The Simple Setup: No set is required. **Bradley** will need a large bag containing a winter coat, scarf, several sheets of newspaper, and a roll of masking tape. **Kid 3** will need a sheet of paper. All actors should wear school clothes.

Puppet Options: You could use puppets for all the roles except **Maria**. Cast a child or adult as **Maria**; the **Bradley** puppet will need her help to put on his coat, scarf, paper, and tape. Downsize these items as needed to fit the **Bradley** puppet. If **Kid 3** is a puppet, crumple his or her sheet of paper ahead of time. If your **Bradley** puppet doesn't have a mouth into which a piece of paper can be stuffed, put double-sided tape on **Kid 3's** piece of paper so it will stick to the **Bradley** puppet's face.

Extra Touches: To make **Bradley** look even sillier in his disguise, give him a coat that's as puffy as possible—perhaps a coat within a coat.

The Characters:
    Bradley, an "undercover" Christian
    Maria, a friendly fellow student
    Kid 1, a sarcastic student
    Kid 2, a curious but dim student
    Kid 3, a student who's in a hurry

*(As the skit begins, **Bradley** enters with a big sack. He looks around nervously. After a pause, **Maria** enters and sees him.)*

Maria: HI! I haven't SEEN you around our school before. Are you NEW here?

Bradley: NO! I mean, YES! I mean…who wants to KNOW?

Maria: I do. I'm MARIA. What's YOUR name?

Bradley: Uh…I don't HAVE one.

Maria: You don't HAVE a name? How do people know what to CALL you?

Bradley: OK, I've GOT a name. But I can't tell you what it IS unless I know I can TRUST you.

Maria: SURE, you can trust me. I'm a NICE PERSON.

Bradley: A WHAT?

Bradley: YES, but are you a...a...

Maria: A WHAT?

Bradley: I can't say it OUT LOUD. Somebody might HEAR. But it starts with a C.

Maria: CUCUMBER? Am I a CUCUMBER?

Bradley: No, THAT'S not it.

Maria: CLOWN?

Bradley: NO.

Maria: CARPENTER ant?

Bradley: NO.

Maria: Uh...CHRISTIAN?

Bradley: SHH! Someone might HEAR you!

Maria: You want to know if I'm a CHRISTIAN?

Bradley: QUIET! Don't say that word OUT LOUD!

Maria: Why NOT?

Bradley: Because the OTHER KIDS will LAUGH at us if they know we're...YOU-KNOW-WHATS. So are YOU a...YOU-KNOW-WHAT?

Maria: YES. But—

Bradley: *(Interrupting)* OK. My name is BRADLEY. If you're a...YOU-KNOW-WHAT, you can HELP me with my DISGUISE.

Maria: DISGUISE?

Bradley: It's in this BAG. *(Pulls a heavy coat and scarf from the bag and starts to put it on.)*

HELP me with this SCARF, WOULD you? *(Wraps the scarf around his face.)*

Maria: WHY are you wearing a COAT and a SCARF? It's EIGHTY DEGREES outside.

Bradley: I've got to COVER UP. I can't let the OTHER KIDS find out I'm a...YOU-KNOW-WHAT!

Maria: You mean...a CHRISTIAN?

Bradley: SHH! I TOLD you not to say that word OUT LOUD!

*(**Kid I** enters the stage.)*

Kid I: HI, Maria! *(Looks at **Bradley**.)* Who's the GEEK? HEY, FROSTY the SNOWMAN, didn't you catch the WEATHER REPORT? It's SUNNY with NO CHANCE of SNOW! *(Laughing, **Kid I** exits the stage.)*

Bradley: SEE? I TOLD you they'd LAUGH if they found out I was a YOU-KNOW-WHAT.

Maria: But THAT wasn't...

Bradley: *(Interrupting)* I've got to do a better job of COVERING UP. Come ON, help me OUT. I've got some PAPER and TAPE in the bag. *(Takes newspaper and masking tape from bag and gives them to **Maria**.)* HERE, tape this PAPER on me, OK?

Maria: What FOR?

Bradley: To COVER ME UP! I can't let the OTHER kids see that I'm a YOU-KNOW-WHAT!

Maria: *(Taping a few sheets of paper over **Bradley**)* This is CRAZY! I don't see why you have to keep it a SECRET that you're a...

Bradley: *(Interrupting)* SHH! Somebody's COMING!

*(**Kid 2** enters the stage.)*

Kid 2: HI, Maria. *(Looks at **Bradley**. Walks back and forth in front of **Bradley**, studying him. Finally speaks to **Bradley**.)* HEY...there's something DIFFERENT about you, ISN'T there?

*(**Bradley** shakes his head quickly.)*

Kid 2: You're not quite LIKE the other kids, ARE you? What IS it that makes you STAND OUT from everybody ELSE? *(Pauses.)* HMM. I can't put my FINGER on it. Maybe it'll come to me LATER. *(Speaking to **Maria**)* See you AROUND, Maria! *(Exits the stage.)*

Bradley: WHEW! THAT was a close call! I'd better COVER UP even more. Give me a HAND, will you? I need more PAPER! More PAPER!

Maria: *(Taping more paper over **Bradley's** head and chest)* This is NUTS, trying to be some kind of UNDERCOVER CHRISTIAN.

Bradley: SHH! You said that WORD!

Maria: How can you even BREATHE with all this STUFF on?

Bradley: UH-oh! Here comes somebody ELSE!

*(**Kid 3** enters the stage, carrying a sheet of paper.)*

Kid 3: HI, Maria! How are YOU?

Maria: Um…OK.

Kid 3: SO how did you do on the MATH TEST?

Maria: OK, I THINK.

Kid 3: It was a HARD one! Well, I guess I can get RID of my STUDY NOTES now. *(Crumples the sheet of paper and stuffs it into **Bradley's** mouth.)*

Bradley: MMFF! HMFF!

Kid 3: It TALKED! That TRASH CAN TALKED!

Maria: Uh…that's NOT a TRASH CAN.

Kid 3: *(Looking more closely at **Bradley**)* OH! SORRY! With all that PAPER and everything, I thought you were a TRASH CAN. *(Speaking to **Maria**)* Well, BYE, Maria. See you AROUND. *(Exits the stage.)*

Bradley: *(Spits out the piece of paper.)* It WORKED! She thought I was a TRASH CAN!

Maria: And you think that's GOOD?

Bradley: It's GREAT! If people think I'm a TRASH CAN, they won't know I'm a…YOU-KNOW-WHAT.

Maria: WELL, Bradley, it was nice to MEET you. But I've got to get to CLASS.

Bradley: OK. But...MARIA?

Maria: YEAH?

Bradley: Where's YOUR disguise?

Maria: I didn't think I NEEDED one. *(Exits the stage.)*

Bradley: Boy, is SHE mixed up! Doesn't she REALIZE that without a COVERUP like MINE, people might make FUN of her? *(Exits the stage, walking awkwardly, barely able to move in all the clothing and paper.)*

● To Talk About:

- Have you ever felt the way Bradley did? If so, when?
- Why do you suppose Maria didn't cover up her faith, too?
- How do some kids try to hide the fact that they're Christians—other than using paper and tape?
- What might happen if every Christian in your school wore an "I'm a Christian" button for a week?
- What are some other ways Christians at your school could show what they believe?

● Other Topical Tie-Ins:

Sharing your faith   Persecution   How Christians can help each other

Fast Forward

Topic: Patience

Scriptures You Might Read: Psalm 27:14; Proverbs 19:11

The Scene: Inside a house

The Simple Setup: You'll need a table with a VCR remote control and a few baking supplies on it—a mixing bowl and spoon would suffice. A sack marked "flour" but filled with confetti or torn paper should be near the table. You'll also need a leaf rake. Actors of either gender could play the roles of **Pepper** and **Terry**, with minor word changes. Let **Mr. McDonald** know that, when he sings the words to the song "John Jacob Jingleheimer Schmidt" backward, he can sing the tune normally to make it easier.

Puppet Options: You could use puppets for all the roles, though you may wish to cast a leader as **Mom** since she must manipulate the spoon and the sack of confetti. **Mr. McDonald** could also be a live actor. Downsize props for puppets—a toy rake and a matchbox-size remote control made of black cardboard with white buttons, for example.

Extra Touches: If you'd like, use a sound effect to indicate when the remote control is working. Any sound will do, but a VCR-type whir or fast, tinny piano music would suggest speed.

The Characters:

> **Pepper,** who's very impatient
> **Terry,** his friend
> **Mr. McDonald,** a neighbor
> **Mom,** Pepper's hard-working mother

*(As the skit begins, **Pepper** is waiting impatiently. After a few seconds, **Terry** enters.)*

Terry:	😊	HI, Pepper! You wanted to SEE me?
Pepper:	😠	YEAH, I wanted to SEE you—THREE MINUTES and TWELVE SECONDS AGO.
Terry:	🙄	Well, I had to WAIT for a RED LIGHT down on the CORNER, and...
Pepper:	😠	*(Interrupting)* You shouldn't WAIT for RED LIGHTS! That makes ME have to wait! And you KNOW how I HATE TO WAIT!

Terry: Yeah, I KNOW. Maybe you need to learn a little PATIENCE, Pepper. The Bible says…

Pepper: *(Interrupting)* PATIENCE? I don't have TIME to learn PATIENCE! And thanks to my new INVENTION, I won't HAVE to!

Terry: INVENTION? YOU invented something? WHAT are you now, a SCIENTIST?

Pepper: That's RIGHT. You can call me…DOCTOR Pepper!

Terry: OK…DOCTOR. Exactly what did you INVENT?

Pepper: It's a SECRET. Are you SURE nobody else is LISTENING?

Terry: No one—except all those KIDS out there.

Pepper: GOOD. My invention is…the HURRY-UP FIVE THOUSAND!

Terry: The HURRY-UP FIVE THOUSAND? What does it DO?

Pepper: It SPEEDS things up so I don't have to WAIT. I HATE TO WAIT!

Terry: So I've HEARD. Can you SHOW me the HURRY-UP FIVE THOUSAND?

Pepper: It's right HERE. *(Picks up a device that looks like a remote control and shows it to **Terry**.)*

Terry: It looks like…a VCR REMOTE CONTROL. There's a button that says "PLAY," one that says "STOP"…

Pepper: *(Interrupting)* FORGET those. THIS is the IMPORTANT one. *(Points at a button on the remote.)*

Terry: *(Reading)* FAST FORWARD?

Pepper: RIGHT!

*(**Mr. McDonald** enters the stage, raking imaginary leaves and softly singing the song, ¨John Jacob Jingle-heimer Schmidt.¨)*

Pepper: See our NEIGHBOR, MR. MCDONALD, raking LEAVES? Watch THIS. *(Points the remote at Mr. McDonald.)* I just push the FAST FORWARD button, and…*(Pushes a button on the remote.)*

Mr. McDonald: *(Suddenly singing very quickly as he rakes at top speed)* "JOHN Jacob Jingleheimer SCHMIDT, HIS name is my name TOO. Whenever we go OUT the people always SHOUT, 'JOHN JACOB JINGLEHEIMER SCHMIDT.' Dah DAH dah DAH dah dah dah…"

*(***Pepper*** again points the remote at **Mr. McDonald** and pushes a button. **Mr. McDonald** freezes.)*

Pepper: SEE? Now he's on PAUSE.

Terry: How'd you DO that?

Pepper: I can even put him on REWIND. *(Points the remote at **Mr. McDonald** and pushes button.)*

McDonald: *(Pretending to push leaves away with the rake while singing the song "backward")* "Dah DAH dah DAH dah dah dah. 'SCHMIDT Jingleheimer Jacob JOHN,' shout ALWAYS people the out go we WHENEVER…"

Pepper: 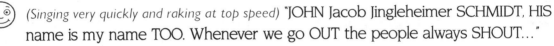 *(Pushing a button on the remote and interrupting)* But the BEST is FAST FORWARD.

Mr. McDonald: *(Singing very quickly and raking at top speed)* "JOHN Jacob Jingleheimer SCHMIDT, HIS name is my name TOO. Whenever we go OUT the people always SHOUT…"

Pepper: 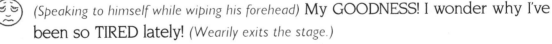 *(Pushing a button on the remote and interrupting)* And back to NORMAL.

Mr. McDonald: *(Speaking to himself while wiping his forehead)* My GOODNESS! I wonder why I've been so TIRED lately! *(Wearily exits the stage.)*

Pepper: Pretty COOL, eh?

Terry: Well…

Pepper: 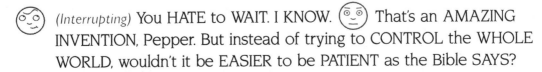 Now whenever I WANT something, I can just SPEED PEOPLE UP so they'll do it RIGHT AWAY. I won't have to wait for ANYTHING anymore! Because I HATE…

Terry: *(Interrupting)* You HATE to WAIT. I KNOW. That's an AMAZING INVENTION, Pepper. But instead of trying to CONTROL the WHOLE WORLD, wouldn't it be EASIER to be PATIENT as the Bible SAYS?

Pepper: No WAY! Now how about a SNACK?

Terry: A SNACK? I guess that would be…

Pepper: *(Interrupting)* Hey, MOM!

*(**Mom** enters the stage.)*

Mom: YES, dear?

Pepper: We'd like some SUGAR COOKIES.

Mom: *(Walking to the table of baking supplies)* I'll be GLAD to make you some, dear. But they'll take about FORTY-FIVE MINUTES.

Pepper: *(Following **Mom** to the table)* Oh, NO they won't.

*(**Pepper** points the remote at **Mom** and pushes a button. **Mom** goes into fast-motion mode, humming quickly and using the spoon and bowl to stir imaginary ingredients at top speed.)*

Pepper: *(Speaking to **Terry**)* Works like a CHARM.

*(**Mom** moves faster and faster. She grabs the open "flour" sack and flings it around, getting as much on the table as in the bowl.)*

Pepper: Uh...MOM? Maybe you'd better...SLOW DOWN...uh...

*(Still humming. **Mom** flings "flour" in **Pepper's** face, not noticing what she's doing.)*

Pepper: MOM! HEY! Slow DOWN!

*(**Mom** flings even more "flour" in **Pepper's** face.)*

Pepper: YUCK! PHEWY! Hey, MOM! *(Fumbles for the remote and points it at **Mom**.)* Got to...STOP her....

*(**Pepper** pushes a button. Suddenly **Mom** stops, then walks backward to exit the stage.)*

Pepper: OOPS! I hit the REWIND button. Can't SEE with this FLOUR in my eyes...

*(**Pepper** points the remote in the direction **Mom** left, but holds it backward without realizing it. **Pepper** pushes the button and suddenly speeds up.)*

Pepper: *(Talking and moving quickly)* Oh, NO! I pointed the remote at MYSELF! Now I'm on FAST FORWARD! *(Points the remote at himself and pushes a button.)* HELP! It's STUCK! I can't slow myself DOWN! *(Walks back and forth quickly, waving the remote.)* What am I gonna DO? What am I gonna DO? What am I gonna DO? What am I gonna DO?

Terry: Uh…maybe when the BATTERIES in your HURRY-UP FIVE THOUSAND RUN DOWN, YOU will TOO! I guess you'll just have to…WAIT!

Pepper: *(Speaking quickly as he exits the stage)* I HATE to WAIT! I HATE to WAIT! I HATE to WAIT! I HATE to WAIT!

Terry: *(Speaking after a pause)* Hmm, it looks like DOCTOR Pepper DID need some PATIENCE AFTER all! *(Exits the stage.)*

● To Talk About:

- If you could make an invention like Pepper's that actually worked, would you? Why or why not?
- Is it most difficult for you to be patient with friends, strangers, parents, God, or yourself? Why?
- How would you answer Terry's question, "Instead of trying to control the whole world, wouldn't it be easier to be patient as the Bible says?" Explain your answer.
- If you were really patient all day tomorrow, what do you think you would lose by the end of the day? What might you gain?

● Other Topical Tie-Ins:

God's control   Selfishness   Letting God meet our needs

The Greatest

Topic: Serving Others

Scriptures You Might Read: Matthew 20:20-28; Philippians 2:4-8

The Scene: A street corner

The Simple Setup: No set is required. All actors may wear casual clothes, though **Grown-up** could be in "Sunday best" if you like. **Grown-up** will need a newspaper and a watch, and **Little Girl** will need two paper cups. Actors of either gender could play all roles, with minor word changes needed if **Grown-up** is a woman or **Little Girl** is a boy.

Puppet Options: You could use puppets for all the roles. If you want to mix puppets and live actors, cast a leader as **Grown-up**. If you use puppets, downsize the props—a small book in place of a newspaper and small paper cups, for example.

Extra Touches: If you'd like, play recorded *Rocky*-type music while **Sam** and **Max** do their exercises.

The Characters:
    Sam, who's very competitive
    Max, who's also very competitive
    Grown-up, an innocent bystander
    Little Girl, who's helpful and polite

*(As the skit begins, **Grown-up** is standing as if waiting for a bus and reading a newspaper. **Sam** and **Max** enter, arguing.)*

Sam: I am!

Max: No, I am!

Sam: You're CRAZY! I REALLY am!

Max: YOU'RE CRAZY because I REALLY am!

Sam: There's only ONE way to settle this. *(Speaking to **Grown-up**)* EXCUSE me, sir.

Grown-up: *(Lowering newspaper)* Yes?

Sam: My FRIEND and I are trying to settle a SMALL but PESKY DISPUTE.

Max: Oh, quit trying to IMPRESS him.

Sam: I am NOT trying to IMPRESS him!

Max: You really ARE!

Sam: I am really NOT!

Grown-up: WHOA! HOLD IT! *(Pauses.)* What is this argument ABOUT, anyway?

Sam: It's about WHICH of us is the GREATEST!

Grown-up: The GREATEST?

Sam: That's RIGHT. And we need someone to SETTLE it for us.

Max: Someone SMART, and someone FAIR.

Sam: Someone about YOUR SIZE, STANDING on the STREET CORNER, reading a NEWSPAPER.

Grown-up: Uh...that would be ME, I guess.

Sam: So you'll DO it?

Grown-up: Well...OK.

Max: GREAT! *(Clears throat.)* I will now PROVE that I am the GREATEST by...making FINGER SHADOWS of a GIANT AFRICAN BUTTERFLY! *(Puts hands together in a butterfly shape and wiggles fingers.)*

Sam: Ha! That's NOTHING! I will now PROVE that I am the GREATEST by...PATTING MY HEAD and RUBBING MY STOMACH at the SAME TIME! *(Pats head and rubs stomach at the same time.)* THERE! Now WHICH of us is the GREATEST?

Grown-up: Well, I really can't TELL yet.

Max: No PROBLEM! I will PROVE that I am the GREATEST by...NAMING ALL THE PLANETS IN THE SOLAR SYSTEM IN ORDER OF THEIR DISTANCE FROM THE SUN! *(Clears throat.)* Mercury, Venus, Earth, Mars, Jupiter, Saturn...

Sam: *(Interrupting)* Too EASY! I'll name ALL THE U.S. STATES IN ABC ORDER... BACKWARD! Wyoming, Wisconsin, West Virginia, Washington, Virginia...

Max: *(Interrupting)* THAT doesn't prove ANYTHING! I'll tell you the SQUARE ROOT of 75,000! It's 273.86127!

Sam: Oh, YEAH? Well, 889 times 998 is 887,222! So NOW who's the greatest?

Grown-up: I wish I could TELL you, but...

Max: *(Interrupting)* OK, THIS will prove I'm the GREATEST. I will now do ONE HUNDRED JUMPING JACKS! *(Begins doing jumping jacks.)* ONE, two, THREE, four...

Sam: What a WIMP! I'll do FIVE HUNDRED TOE TOUCHES! *(Begins touching toes.)* ONE and two and...

Max: *(Speaking as if short of breath)* YEAH? Well, I'll do THREE THOUSAND PUSH-UPS! *(Begins doing push-ups.)* One...two...

Sam: *(Also speaking as if short of breath)* And I'll do TEN MILLION SIT-UPS! *(Begins doing sit-ups.)* ONE...TWO...

*(**Sam** and **Max** do exercises as fast as they can, mixing up the kinds of exercises they're doing, getting more and more exhausted. Finally they collapse on the floor.)*

Max: UGH!

Sam: Can't...go...ON...

Max: Must decide...who is...the GREATEST...

*(**Little Girl** enters with two paper cups.)*

Little Girl: PARDON me, but I THOUGHT you two must be AWFULLY THIRSTY. I have a LEMONADE STAND down the street, and I thought you might like a DRINK.

*(**Little Girl** gives a cup to **Sam** and a cup to **Max**; they take a drink and sigh, then collapse again.)*

Little Girl: Well, I'd better get BACK. Hope you guys FEEL better! *(Exits the stage.)*

Grown-up: And...we have a WINNER!

Sam: HUH?

Max: Winner of WHAT?

Grown-up: I finally know who's the GREATEST!

Sam: You mean ME?

Max: ME?

Grown-up: No, I mean that GIRL with the LEMONADE. SHE'S the greatest!

Max: But SHE didn't do any PUSH-UPS!

Sam: She didn't even NAME the STATE CAPITALS!

Max: She CAN'T be the greatest!

Grown-up: You're FORGETTING what JESUS said: "Whoever wants to become GREAT among you must be your SERVANT."

Sam: SERVANT?

Max: You mean…being the GREATEST is being the BEST at HELPING OTHER PEOPLE?

Grown-up: EXACTLY! *(Looks at watch.)* Well, I have to be GOING. Glad we could SETTLE this little ARGUMENT. *(Exits the stage.)*

Sam: SO are you going to try being the BEST SERVANT?

Max: Are you KIDDING? HELPING OTHER PEOPLE makes you…too TIRED!

*(**Sam** and **Max** crawl off the stage.)*

● **To Talk About:**

- What are some other ways Sam and Max might have tried to prove they were the greatest?
- Who's the greatest person in your school? Why?
- Which would make you more tired: mowing your own lawn or mowing the lawn of an elderly person who can't do it?
- Do you think serving others is harder than serving yourself? Why?
- How has one of the following been a servant to you?
  - a friend? someone you hardly knew? a parent? Jesus?
- How could you follow that person's example?

● **Other Topical Tie-Ins:**

| Humility | Selfishness | Competition |

Gross Bumps

Topic: Fear

Scriptures You Might Read: Psalms 23; 91:2-6

The Scene: A forest at night

The Simple Setup: Place a few pieces of wood at center stage to suggest a campfire. If possible, put a red or orange light under the wood. **Kid 1** will need a backpack containing at least three books; each book should have a homemade "Gross Bumps" cover (see script for the titles of the books). All actors may wear casual clothes.

Puppet Options: You could use puppets for all the roles. If you use a puppet for **Kid 1**, make miniature "Gross Bumps" books, and have the puppet "read" from the back covers rather than trying to hold the books open. If you want to mix puppets and live actors, cast a child or leader as **Kid 1.**

Extra Touches: For a spooky effect, train a dim blue light on the stage.

The Characters:

    Kid 1, a fan of scary books
    Kid 2, who's convinced he or she is fearless
    Kid 3, who's similar to **Kid 2**

*(As the skit begins, **Kids 1, 2,** and **3** are sitting around a campfire.)*

Kid 1: 🙂 WOW, it sure is DARK and SPOOKY out here in the WOODS, huh?

Kid 2: 😌 YEAH, but I'm not SCARED.

Kid 3: 😌 Me NEITHER.

Kid 1: 😟 So you think we did the RIGHT THING by CAMPING out here with all the MONSTERS and WILD ANIMALS and all?

Kid 2: 😏 Oh, COME ON! There's no such THING as MONSTERS!

Kid 3: 😏 And the only WILD ANIMAL I've seen is that BIG RED AND ORANGE SNAKE CRAWLING UP THE BACK OF YOUR NECK.

Kid 1: WHAT? WHERE?

Kid 3: Just KIDDING!

Kid 1: OK, smarty. We'll SEE who's got something to be SCARED of. *(Reaches into backpack and pulls out books.)* I brought…"GROSS BUMPS" BOOKS.

Kid 2: "GROSS BUMPS?" You mean those HORROR BOOKS by FRANK N. STINE?

Kid 3: THEY aren't scary!

Kid 1: Oh YEAH? Let's see how BRAVE you are when I read you part of NIGHT OF THE LIVING DOOFUS! *(Chooses a book and reads in a spooky voice.)* "It was a DARK and CREEPY NIGHT. Just above the TREES, the FULL MOON sailed like the EYE of a FISH floating in a MUD PUDDLE. Just beyond the HILLS, a WOLF HOWLED like a CIRCUS CLOWN whose FOOT had just been run over by a GOLF CART. Just below the…"

Kid 2: *(Interrupting)* THAT'S not scary!

Kid 3: *(Yawning)* YEAH. You're putting me to SLEEP.

Kid 1: Well, you'll CHANGE YOUR TUNE when I read you some of *Welcome to Stinky House.* *(Chooses another book and reads in a spooky voice.)* "The GHOST of GRANNY GREEN floated down the STAIRS, her LONG DRESS dragging on the STEPS like the BROKEN ARM of a WRESTLING OCTOPUS. The ghost came CLOSER, CLOSER, until I could feel her ICE-COLD BREATH, as COLD as ICE CUBES in an ICE CUBE TRAY on an ICY COLD MORNING in the country of ICELAND…"

Kid 2: *(Interrupting)* OOH! I'm SO terrified!

Kid 3: Hey, YOU can't scare us with THAT stuff. WE know there's NO SUCH THING as GHOSTS.

Kid 2: BESIDES, we know that GOD will take care of us.

Kid 3: YEAH! We're CHRISTIANS!

Kid 1: Is that RIGHT? Well, THIS will send shivers down your spine! It's from *The Curse of Camp Carving Knife!* *(Chooses another book and reads in a spooky voice.)* "Out of the SHADOWS came the CRAZY MAN, bent on HUNTING me until I couldn't GO ON. I could see his CRAZY RED EYES—eyes as RED as the NOSE on the face of the CLOWN whose FOOT had just been run over by a GOLF CART, as I mentioned in "Gross Bumps" number 179, *Night of the Living Doofus...*"

Kid 2:   *(Interrupting)* Give it UP! YOU can't scare US!

Kid 3:   "Fear NOT!" That's what the BIBLE says.

Kid 2:   "Even though I walk through the VALLEY of the SHADOW OF DEATH, I will FEAR NO EVIL." The Bible says THAT, too!

Kid 3:   So WE'RE not afraid of ANYTHING!

Kid 1:   Not even...BATS?

Kid 2:   NO.

Kid 1:   VAMPIRES?

Kid 3:   NOPE.

Kid 1:   MUMMIES?

Kid 2:   NO.

Kid 1:   ZOMBIES?

Kid 3:   No WAY.

Kid 1:   OK. I give UP. I guess you really DO believe that GOD will PROTECT you.

Kid 2:   ANYPLACE...

Kid 3:   ANY TIME.

Kid 1:   *(Holding up a book)* SO, speaking of BOOKS, what books are YOU reading for your BOOK REPORTS on Monday?

Kid 2:   BOOK REPORTS?

Kid 3:   MONDAY?

Kid 1:   YEAH. For Miss GRUBER'S class.

Kid 2:   But I can't do a BOOK REPORT! You have to get up in front of the

WHOLE CLASS and TALK! If I do THAT, I'll FAINT!

Kid 3: And I can't write one by MONDAY! I haven't even STARTED!

Kid 2: *(Standing)* I'm going to FAINT!

Kid 3: *(Standing)* I'm going to FLUNK!

Kids 2 and 3: *(Speaking together)* AARGH! *(Run off the stage.)*

Kid 1: *(Pauses.)* HMM. Not scared of ANYTHING, eh? *(Putting books in the backpack)* Reminds me of "Gross Bumps" number 398: *Attack of the Anti-Social Studies Teacher.* *(Starts to leave.)* Or was it number 726: *Nightmare on Report Card Street*? Or was it... *(Exits the stage.)*

● **To Talk About:**

- What used to scare you but doesn't anymore? What changed?
- Does being a Christian make a difference in how scared you get? Should it? Why or why not?
- Do you think it's a good idea to read scary books and watch scary movies? Why or why not?
- Do you think God is afraid of anything? If not, what does that tell you about being afraid yourself?

● **Other Topical Tie-Ins:**

Entertainment choices   Relating to non-Christians   Trusting God

Highway to Heaven

Topic: How to Get to Heaven

Scriptures You Might Read: John 3:16; 14:1-6

The Scene: A school parking lot

The Simple Setup: This skit spoofs the *Magic School Bus* TV series. Use four chairs in single file to suggest a bus, and have the chairs facing stage left. Use the front chair as the driver's seat. Have **Ms. Drizzle** wear a brightly colored dress with lots of cloud and star shapes (fabric or paper) fastened to it. The other actors should wear school clothes, and **Alfie** should add a backward baseball cap. **Ms. Drizzle** should sound bubbly, almost singsong—except when she's mad. When the script calls for noisemaker sound effects, have offstage helpers use party favors, spinning ratchet noisemakers, slide whistles, or other sounds of your choice.

Puppet Options: You could use puppets for all the roles—or you could cast a leader as **Ms. Drizzle**. If you use puppets, skip the chairs; the **Ms. Drizzle** puppet can show her ire by growling rather then frowning and stamping her feet.

Extra Touches: If you have time, add details that make the characters look more like their *Magic School Bus* counterparts (for reference, see the videos or books based on the TV series). You might give **Ms. Drizzle** an upswept, frizzy red wig, for instance; **Alfie** could have a big "A" on his shirt; **Ronald** could wear large, round glasses.

The Characters:

    Ms. Drizzle, a dramatic and excitable teacher
    Alfie, who's fairly normal
    Dorothy Em, who's serious and precise
    Ronald, who's nervous about everything

*(As the skit begins, all characters except **Ms. Drizzle** are onstage, standing outside the "bus.")*

Alfie: So where do you think we'll be going on our FIELD TRIP TODAY? When you're part of the MAGIC SCHOOL BUNCH, you never KNOW!

Dorothy Em: At my OLD school, we only went on NORMAL field trips…like to the DRINKING FOUNTAIN!

Ronald: Oh, I KNEW I should have STAYED IN BED today! Except that my

MATTRESS was on FIRE...

Alfie: Hey, LOOK! Here comes MS. DRIZZLE!

(**Ms. Drizzle** *enters the stage.*)

Ms. Drizzle: Good MORNING, class!

Alfie, Dorothy Em, and **Ronald:** *(Speaking together)* Good MORNING, Ms. Drizzle!

Alfie: Ms. Drizzle, where are we GOING on our FIELD TRIP today?

Ms. Drizzle: I'm GLAD you asked that QUESTION, Alfie! That's the ONLY way you'll LEARN!

Alfie: *(Pauses.)* SO...what's the ANSWER?

Ms. Drizzle: Well, Alfie, I'll give you a HINT: It has PEARLY GATES and GOLDEN STREETS!

Alfie: DISNEY WORLD? We're going to DISNEY WORLD?

Ms. Drizzle: Nice TRY, Alfie. But you're WRONG, WRONG, WRONG! *(Pauses.)* ALFIE, DOROTHY EM, RONALD...we're going to...HEAVEN!

Alfie: HEAVEN?

Dorothy Em: But at my OLD school, we were NEVER allowed to enter the AFTERLIFE!

Ms. Drizzle: Don't WORRY, Dorothy Em. We'll be PERFECTLY SAFE!

Ronald: I KNEW I should have STAYED HOME today...except that a GAS PIPE BLEW UP and TORE MY HOUSE TO BITS.

Ms. Drizzle: Now, RONALD, don't be such a SCAREDY-CAT. Take that FIRST STEP! Get MESSED UP! Make HUGE MISTAKES that go on your PERMANENT RECORD!

Alfie: Uh...Ms. Drizzle...how are we going to GET to heaven?

Ms. Drizzle: I'm glad you asked that QUESTION, Alfie...although it DOES show that you're not very BRIGHT. We're going on the BUS, of course! That's what the MAGIC SCHOOL BUNCH ALWAYS does!

Alfie: But how can a BUS get us to HEAVEN?

Ms. Drizzle: COME now, Alfie. How hard can it BE? This bus goes anywhere I SAY it can! So HOP ON, everybody!

(All enter the "bus" and sit on chairs, with Ms. Drizzle in front.)

Ms. Drizzle: SEAT BELTS ON, everyone!

Alfie: Uh...this is a BUS, Ms. Drizzle. It doesn't HAVE seat belts.

Ms. Drizzle: I KNEW that! *(Pauses.)* BRACE yourselves! I'm going to THROW A SWITCH and PULL SOME LEVERS! *(Pretends to manipulate imaginary controls.)*

(Offstage helpers sound the noisemakers.)

Alfie: Ooh, LOOK! The bus is CHANGING SHAPE! It looks like a big yellow HAPPY FACE!

Ms. Drizzle: Right you ARE, Alfie! That's because the way to get to heaven is...by BEING NICE!

Dorothy Em: Being NICE? But according to my RESEARCH...

Ms. Drizzle: *(Interrupting)* No TIME for RESEARCH, Dorothy Em! Put on your best SMILE, everyone! Here we GO! *(Grabs an imaginary steering wheel and turns an imaginary key. After a pause, frowns.)* I said, "HERE WE GO!" *(Again grabs steering wheel turns key. Then frowns again.)*

Alfie: Nothing's HAPPENING! We're just SITTING here like a BIG YELLOW TENNIS BALL!

Ms. Drizzle: Thank you for sharing that COLORFUL DESCRIPTION, Alfie. But NEXT time, keep it to YOURSELF!

Alfie: Maybe being NICE ISN'T the way to heaven.

Ms. Drizzle: All RIGHT! No PROBLEM! I'll just PUSH SOME OTHER BUTTONS. *(Pretends to manipulate imaginary controls.)*

(Offstage helpers sound the noisemakers.)

Alfie: LOOK! The bus is CHANGING SHAPE again! Now it looks like...a giant yellow WORK GLOVE!

Ms. Drizzle: That's because the way to get to heaven is...by DOING GOOD DEEDS!

Dorothy Em: GOOD DEEDS? But according to my RESEARCH…

Ms. Drizzle: *(Interrupting)* We don't NEED no RESEARCH! Hold ON, everybody! Here we GO! *(Grabs the steering wheel and turns the key. Frowns, then tries again, then stamps her feet.)*

Alfie: We're not MOVING! We're just SITTING here like a big yellow…WORK GLOVE!

Ms. Drizzle: Oh, that's BRILLIANT, Alfie! Remind me to give you an "A" for ORIGINALITY! *(Pauses.)* OK, so GOOD DEEDS AREN'T the way to heaven. I've got ONE MORE idea. I'll just set these CONTROLS… *(Manipulates imaginary controls.)*

(Offstage helper sounds the noisemakers.)

Alfie: WOW! The bus is CHANGING SHAPE AGAIN! It looks like…a CHURCH!

Ms. Drizzle: Don't tell the SCHOOL BOARD. But MAYBE, just MAYBE, the way to get to heaven is by going to CHURCH.

Dorothy Em: CHURCH? But according to my RESEARCH…

Ms. Drizzle: *(Interrupting)* THAT'S enough, Dorothy Em! Here we GO! *(Tries key again.)* AARGH! *(Tries once more, then stamps feet repeatedly.)* You stupid pile of JUNK! I should have pushed you over a cliff YEARS ago!

Ronald: I KNEW I should have STAYED AT SCHOOL today…except that they were serving that GREEN AND ORANGE MYSTERY MEAT in the LUNCHROOM.

Dorothy Em: EXCUSE me, Ms. Drizzle, but according to my RESEARCH, there's only ONE WAY to get to heaven.

Ms. Drizzle: And what's THAT, Miss KNOW-IT-ALL?

Dorothy Em: Oh, it's not MY idea. It's in the BIBLE. The way to get to HEAVEN is to TRUST JESUS to TAKE you there.

Ms. Drizzle: WHAT? *(Pushing buttons on imaginary dashboard)* But I don't HAVE any BUTTONS for that!

Dorothy Em: That's because we can't GET there on our OWN.

Ms. Drizzle: IMPOSSIBLE! If that were TRUE, I would KNOW about it! I'm the TEACHER!

Alfie: Uh…Ms. Drizzle…it's OK if you need to ask QUESTIONS. That's the only way to LEARN, after all.

Ms. Drizzle: AARGH! I don't ASK questions, I ANSWER them! *(Stands.)* This field trip is CANCELED! I'm going back to my OLD job! *(Leaves "bus" and exits the stage.)*

Alfie: BOY, I guess the "MAGIC" is GONE, huh?

Dorothy Em: Looks like we won't be having any FIELD TRIPS for a while.

Ronald: I KNEW I should have stayed... Hey, WAIT a minute. I don't have to SAY that anymore! *(Stands.)* This is GREAT! I was so TIRED of SAYING that all the time!

Alfie: *(Standing)* And we were tired of HEARING it.

Dorothy Em: *(Standing)* Well, we'd better get back to CLASS. I wonder who our NEW TEACHER will be.

(They start to exit the stage.)

Alfie: Maybe that guy who always wears a SWEATER and keeps talking about his NEIGHBORHOOD...

Ronald: Or that PURPLE DINOSAUR...

Dorothy Em: Or that WEIRD DOG who keeps TALKING TO HIMSELF. WHAT'S his name? FISHBONE?

(They all exit the stage.)

⬤ **To Talk About:**

- What three ways did Ms. Drizzle try to get to heaven? Why didn't they work?
- Which do you think most people would rather do to get to heaven: Be nice, do good deeds, go to church, or trust Jesus to take them? Why?
- Read John 14:6. How could you explain to your best friend what this verse is talking about?
- If you went on a "field trip" to heaven, what would you most want to see? Why?

⬤ **Other Topical Tie-Ins:**

| Faith | Death | Deciding to follow Jesus |

Home Alone, Too

Topic: Obeying Parents

Scriptures You Might Read: Ephesians 6:1-3; Colossians 3:20

The Scene: A living room

The Simple Setup: The only set you'll need is a small table at one side of the stage with a pencil on it. You'll also need a piece of paper, two small pillows, two arm slings (bandannas tied at the shoulder work well), and several adhesive bandages. All actors may wear casual clothes; **Brother** and **Sister** should wear shirts loose enough that small pillows can be stuffed under them during the skit. Have an adult offstage to help **Brother** and **Sister** add pillows, slings, and bandages at the appropriate times. To make the crashing sounds, have an offstage helper drop a large box of pots and pans or something else that will clatter noisily. With minor word changes, actors of either gender could play all roles.

Puppet Options: You could use puppets for all the roles. If you want to involve a leader, cast her as **Mom** (or cast *him* as **Dad**). If you use puppets, use the behind-the-scenes area under the puppet stage as the "kitchen." Inflate the **Brother** and **Sister** puppets' abdomens with balls of masking tape, sticky side out so they adhere to the puppets. You won't need the table if you use puppets; just put the pencil in any convenient spot.

Extra Touches: If you'd like, add a sofa or overstuffed chair to help identify the location as a living room.

The Characters:

> **Brother,** who wants to break the rules
> **Sister,** his similar sibling
> **Mom,** their mother

*(As the skit begins, **Mom** is talking to **Brother** and **Sister**.)*

Mom: OK, kids. I'm just going to be gone for FIVE MINUTES. You can take care of yourselves for THAT long, RIGHT?

Sister and Brother: *(Speaking together)* YES, Mom!

Mom: All RIGHT. But REMEMBER: FOLLOW THE RULES posted on the REFRIGERATOR.

Sister and
Brother: (*Speaking together*) YES, Mom!

Mom: See you in FIVE MINUTES. BYE!

Sister and
Brother: (*Speaking together*) BYE, Mom!

(**Mom** *exits the stage.* **Sister** *watches through an imaginary front window.*)

Brother: Is she GONE yet?

Sister: Sure IS!

Brother: GREAT! We're finally...

Sister and
Brother: (*Speaking together*) ...HOME ALONE!

Brother: This is our BIG CHANCE to do ANYTHING WE WANT!

Sister: YEAH, like...

Sister and
Brother: (*Speaking together*) ...BREAKING ALL THE RULES ON THE REFRIGERATOR!

Brother: I'll go get the LIST. (*Exits the stage.*)

Sister: HURRY! We've only got FIVE MINUTES!

(**Brother** *returns with a piece of paper.*)

Brother: Here it IS! Let's see if we can break ALL THE RULES before she comes BACK!

Sister: (*Looking at list and reading*) "RULE NUMBER ONE: NO SWEET SNACKS between MEALS."

Brother: Oh, BOY! I can hardly WAIT to break THIS one! Let's go in the KITCHEN and eat all the SWEET STUFF we can FIND!

(**Brother** *puts the list on the table.* **Brother** *and* **Sister** *exit the stage, then call out the following lines from offstage while making loud chewing noises. While the actors are offstage, a helper helps them stuff pillows under their shirts.*)

Sister: Mmm...CANDY BARS!

Brother: Yum...PEANUT BUTTER COOKIES!

Sister: Ooh...STRAWBERRY ICE CREAM!

Brother: Mmm...a WHOLE BAG OF CHOCOLATES left over from HALLOWEEN TWO YEARS AGO!

Sister: Yum...FROSTED DOUGHNUTS with SPRINKLES, MAPLE SYRUP, and GUMMY WORMS!

Brother: Ooh...a TWENTY-POUND BAG OF SUGAR!

*(After making a few more noisy eating sounds, **Brother** and **Sister** enter the stage, holding their huge stomachs.)*

Sister: OH, I don't FEEL so good.

Brother: Me NEITHER. But we'd better HURRY! We've got MORE RULES TO BREAK before MOM gets back.

Sister: *(Picks up the piece of paper and reads.)* "RULE NUMBER TWO: NO CLIMBING on the KITCHEN COUNTERS."

Brother: *(Holding his stomach)* OK, here GOES.

Sister: OH, not so FAST! I've got to move SLOWLY or I'll POP!

*(**Sister** puts the list on the table. **Brother** and **Sister** exit the stage, then call out the following lines from offstage. While the actors are offstage, a helper puts bandages on their faces and puts their arms in slings.)*

Brother: OOF! It's hard to get UP here when I'm so FULL.

Sister: You're telling ME.

Brother: UH-oh!

Sister: Look OUT!

(Offstage helper makes a loud crashing sound.)

Brother: OW!

Sister: You knocked over the DISHES!

Brother: Well, YOU knocked over the...

(Offstage helper interrupts with loud crashing sound.)

Sister: OUCH!

Brother: NOW look what you did!

Sister: Look what YOU did!

Brother: Let's get OUT of here!

*(**Brother** and **Sister** enter the stage, holding their stomachs and patting their sore arms.)*

Brother: OHH...

Sister: OHH...

Brother: How many RULES do we have left to BREAK?

Sister: Just ONE. But MOM will be back any MINUTE.

Brother: *(Picks up the list from the table and reads.)* "RULE NUMBER THREE: NO PLAYING WITH MATCHES."

Sister: MATCHES? Oh, NO!

Brother: I don't even WANT to play with matches!

Sister: We might BURN THE HOUSE DOWN!

Brother: But if we follow the RULES, we'll be...

Sister and
Brother: *(Speaking together)* ...OBEYING OUR PARENTS!

Sister: *(Pauses.)* Maybe that's not a bad IDEA.

Brother: OHH, maybe you're RIGHT.

Sister: OOH, I think I'll go to BED.

Brother: Me, TOO—right after I leave a NOTE for MOM.

*(**Brother** picks up the pencil from the table and scribbles on the piece of paper as **Sister** watches over his shoulder.)*

Sister: YEAH. Good IDEA.

*(**Brother** puts the note on the table. Groaning, **Brother** and **Sister** stagger off the stage. After a pause, **Mom** enters the stage.)*

Mom: HELLO! I'm BACK! *(Looks around.)* HMM, I wonder where they WENT. *(Sees the note, picks it up, and reads it aloud.)* "DEAR MOM, HERE is a new RULE for YOU: PLEASE don't EVER leave us HOME ALONE AGAIN!" *(Pauses.)* I wonder what THAT'S all about!

*(Scratching her chin, **Mom** exits the stage.)*

● **To Talk About:**
- In real life, are children more eager to break rules when parents aren't around? Why or why not?
- Have you ever broken a rule and been sorry about it later? What happened?
- What are the top three rules in your home—written or unwritten? How and why do you think these rules were formed?
- If you were a parent, how would you help your children obey the rules when you weren't around? Would you mention that God is always with us? Why or why not?

● **Other Topical Tie-Ins:**

Temptation   Obeying God's rules   Listening to wisdom

I Do Not Like That Sunday School

Topic: Why Church Is Important

Scriptures You Might Read: Psalm 122:1; Hebrews 10:25

The Scene: Outdoors

The Simple Setup: This is a spoof of the Dr. Seuss classic *Green Eggs and Ham*. The only set you'll need is three chairs to represent the inside of a car—two chairs for the front seat, where **Dad** and **Mom** sit when the time comes, and one chair for the back seat, where **Kid** will sit. All actors should wear clothes appropriate for your church, and **Mom** and **Dad** should also wear watches. An actor of either gender could play the role of **Kid**, with minor word changes.

Puppet Options: You could use puppets for all the roles. If you want to mix puppets and live actors, use a puppet for **Kid** and actors for **Mom** and **Dad**.

Extra Touches: If you'd like, accent the Dr. Seuss quality of the skit by adding cartoonish costume accessories—a giant bow tie, big eyeglasses, a polka-dot dress, or Cat in the Hat headgear, for example.

The Characters:
 Mom, who's trying hard to please **Kid**
 Dad, who's also trying hard
 Kid, who's being hard to please

*(As the skit begins, **Kid** stands at center stage, pouting.)*

Kid: 😠 That MOM and DAD!
 That MOM and DAD!
 I DO NOT LIKE that Mom and Dad!

*(**Mom** and **Dad** enter the stage.)*

Mom: 🙄 Will you come to SUNDAY SCHOOL?

Kid: 😝 I do not LIKE that Sunday school.
 I do not LIKE it. It's not COOL.

Dad: 🙄 Would you like to join your CLASS?

Kid: I would NOT like to join my class.
On Sunday school I'll take a PASS.
I do not LIKE that Sunday school.
I do not LIKE it. It's not COOL.

Mom: Would you like to COMB your HAIR?
Would you like to SAY a PRAYER?

Kid: I do not WANT to comb my hair.
I do not WANT to say a prayer
Or SIT FOR AN HOUR on a CHAIR.
For SUNDAY SCHOOL, I do not CARE.
I do not LIKE that Sunday school.
I do not LIKE it. It's not COOL.

Dad: Would you do it if we ROARED?
Would you do it for the LORD?

Kid: Not if you ROARED,
Not for the LORD.
I would be BORED out of my GOURD.
Don't let me hear another PEEP,
For Sunday school puts me to SLEEP.
I do not LIKE that Sunday school.
I do not LIKE it. It's not COOL.

Mom: *(Pointing at the three-chair "car.")* Will you get into the CAR?
GO now, GO now, CHURCH is FAR.

Kid: I will NOT get into the car.

Dad: You may LIKE it. You will SEE.
You may LIKE it, just like ME.

*(**Dad** tries pushing **Kid** into the car.)*

Kid: I would NOT like it. Set me FREE!
Not in the CAR! You LET ME BE!
I do NOT want to hear a tale
About that JONAH and the WHALE.
I do not want to make a CRAFT
Like POPSICLE STICKS that form a RAFT.

I do not LIKE that Sunday school.
I do not LIKE it. It's not COOL.

*(**Dad** stops trying to push **Kid** into the car.)*

Mom: A TREAT!

Dad: A TREAT!

Mom: A TREAT!

Dad: A TREAT!

Mom: Would you if you'd get a TREAT,
Something GOOD and STICKY-SWEET?

Kid: Not for a TREAT, not for a FEE,
Not in the CAR—you LET ME BE!

Dad: WOULD you, COULD you, if we say
You'll be GROUNDED every DAY
If you don't get in that CAR
And go to where your CLASSMATES are?

*(Still pouting. **Kid** gets into the back seat of the car. **Mom** and **Dad** get into the front seats. **Dad** steers an imaginary wheel as if driving.)*

Kid: Yeah, I'll GO to SUNDAY SCHOOL.
But I won't LIKE it. It's not COOL.
I may not throw a HISSY FIT,
But I won't LIKE it—not one BIT!

Mom: You've never BEEN to Sunday school!

Kid: But I won't LIKE it. It's not COOL.

*(**Dad** stops driving.)*

Mom: OK, we're HERE! Let's go INSIDE.

Kid: I'd rather try to RUN and HIDE.
I'm going to hate it ALL, you know.
I'd rather eat a BUG than go.

I will not like the way they LOOK.
I will not like their STORYBOOK.
I will not like the TEACHING CREW.
I will not like the stuff they DO.
I will not like the SONGS they SING.
I will not like a SINGLE THING.
I do not LIKE that Sunday school.
I do not LIKE it. It's not COOL.

Dad: You do not LIKE it,
So you SAY.

Mom: TRY it! TRY it!
And you MAY!

Dad and **Mom:** *(Speaking together)* TRY it and you MAY, we say.

Kid: All RIGHT!
If you will LET ME BE,
I will TRY it. You will SEE.

(**Kid** *gets out of the car and exits the stage.* **Mom** *and* **Dad** *get out and wait nervously, looking at their watches.*)

Mom: I WONDER what he's doing NOW.

Dad: Calm DOWN, dear. Don't have a COW.

(**Kid** *returns.*)

Kid: SAY! I LIKE that Sunday school!
I DO! In fact, it's kind of COOL!
I think I was AFRAID, you see,
that SUNDAY SCHOOL would not like ME.

Mom: You say the others LIKE you, then?

Dad: And you'd like to go AGAIN?

Kid: I used to think you were a FREAK
If you showed up here each WEEK.
But since I've TRIED it, I must SAY,
I'd like to come back every DAY!

Mom: Well, that might be TOO MUCH for US.
Perhaps we'll send you on a BUS.

Kid: SUNDAY SCHOOL is not so BAD.
THANK you, THANK you, Mom and Dad!

(**Kid** *exits the stage.*)

Dad: Or we could send him on a TRAIN.

Mom: Or we could send him on a PLANE.

(**Mom** *and* **Dad** *walk toward exit as they talk.*)

Dad: Or we could send him here by BOAT.

Mom: Or riding on a MOUNTAIN GOAT.

(**Mom** *and* **Dad** *exit the stage.*)

● To Talk About:

- Why do you suppose the kid thought Sunday school wasn't cool?
- If you wanted your son or daughter to go to church and he or she didn't want to, what would you do?
- If someone had never been to our Sunday school group, what might scare him or her most about visiting? What could we do about that?
- If you never went to church again, how do you think it would affect you after a month? a year? ten years?

● Other Topical Tie-Ins:

Obeying parents   Welcoming visitors   Listening

In the Dark

Topic: Faith

Scriptures You Might Read: Luke 17:5-6; Hebrews 11:1

The Scene: A school gym

The Simple Setup: No set is required. Each actor will need a roll of crepe paper. All actors should wear casual clothes. Have a helper offstage be prepared to flick the room lights on and off to mark both the start and end of the "blackout"; the lights should stay on during the blackout, of course, so the audience can see the action. (Note: If you'd like, change the two Valentine's Day references so that the skit refers to another holiday.)

Puppet Options: You could use puppets for both roles. If you want to cast a child or a leader, use him or her in the part of **Kid 2**.

Extra Touches: If you can manipulate your lighting sufficiently, use only a blue light during the blackout.

The Characters:
    Kid 1, who only believes what he or she sees
    Kid 2, who's open to other possibilities

*(As the skit begins, **Kids 1** and **2** enter, carrying crepe paper. They walk to opposite ends of the stage and look around.)*

Kid 1:   😟 UH-oh. This GYM is BIGGER than I THOUGHT.

Kid 2:   😧 YEAH! How are we supposed to DECORATE this whole thing for the VALENTINE'S DAY PARTY?

Kid 1:   ☹️ We'll need about TWO MILES of CREPE PAPER.

Kid 2:   😧 And I only brought ONE mile.

Kid 1:   🙂 So go back HOME and get ANOTHER mile.

Kid 2:   😧 No WAY! It's DARK out there.

Kid 1:   😑 Oh, you're such a…

(Offstage helper suddenly flashes the lights off and on. **Kids 1** *and* **2** *start to feel their way around as if they're in the dark.)*

Kid 2: HEY! What HAPPENED?

Kid 1: The LIGHTS went out! It must be a POWER FAILURE. I can't see a THING.

Kid 2: Neither can I.

Kid 1: This is CREEPY. *(Pause)* Where ARE you, ANYWAY?

Kid 2: Over HERE.

Kid 1: WHERE?

Kid 2: Well, I don't KNOW exactly, but I'm right where I was when the LIGHTS went out.

Kid 1: I don't know whether to BELIEVE you.

Kid 2: Whether to BELIEVE me? What are you TALKING about?

Kid 1: How do I know you're telling the TRUTH?

Kid 2: Of COURSE I'm telling the truth!

Kid 1: But I can't SEE you. And SEEING is BELIEVING.

Kid 2: You can't SEE me because the LIGHTS are out. But I'm still HERE.

Kid 1: So YOU say.

Kid 2: If I WEREN'T here, how could I be TALKING to you?

Kid 1: Maybe you're NOT talking to me. Maybe you're just something I MADE UP in my MIND.

Kid 2: Was I just in your mind THIRTY SECONDS AGO, when you could still SEE me?

Kid 1: I don't REMEMBER. THIRTY SECONDS is a LONG TIME.

Kid 2: LOOK. HOW LONG have we KNOWN each other?

Kid 1: Uh, about FOUR YEARS?

Kid 2: EXACTLY. And in ALL that time, have I ever LIED to you?

Kid 1:		Um, I guess NOT.
Kid 2:		So you can TRUST me, right?
Kid 1:		Well, I could until the LIGHTS went out.
Kid 2:		What does THAT have to do with it? Whether the lights are ON or OFF, I'm still the same PERSON.
Kid 1:		But you're INVISIBLE! I can't believe in a person who's INVISIBLE!
Kid 2:		Why NOT?
Kid 1:		Because people would think I was CRAZY!
Kid 2:		WHY?
Kid 1:		Because things you can't SEE aren't REAL.
Kid 2:		Can you see CELLS? Can you see the WIND? Can you see GEORGE WASHINGTON?
Kid 1:		I can't see ANYTHING! The LIGHTS are out!
Kid 2:		OK, HERE'S what you need to do. You need to have FAITH in me.
Kid 1:		FAITH? What's THAT?
Kid 2:		It's being SURE of what you can't SEE.
Kid 1:		Well then, I can't HAVE faith because I can't SEE it.
Kid 2:		So if you can't SEE something, it doesn't EXIST?
Kid 1:		RIGHT.
Kid 2:		Can you see YOURSELF?
Kid 1:		Uh…NO.
Kid 2:		Then you're not THERE.
Kid 1:		HMM, I guess I'm NOT.

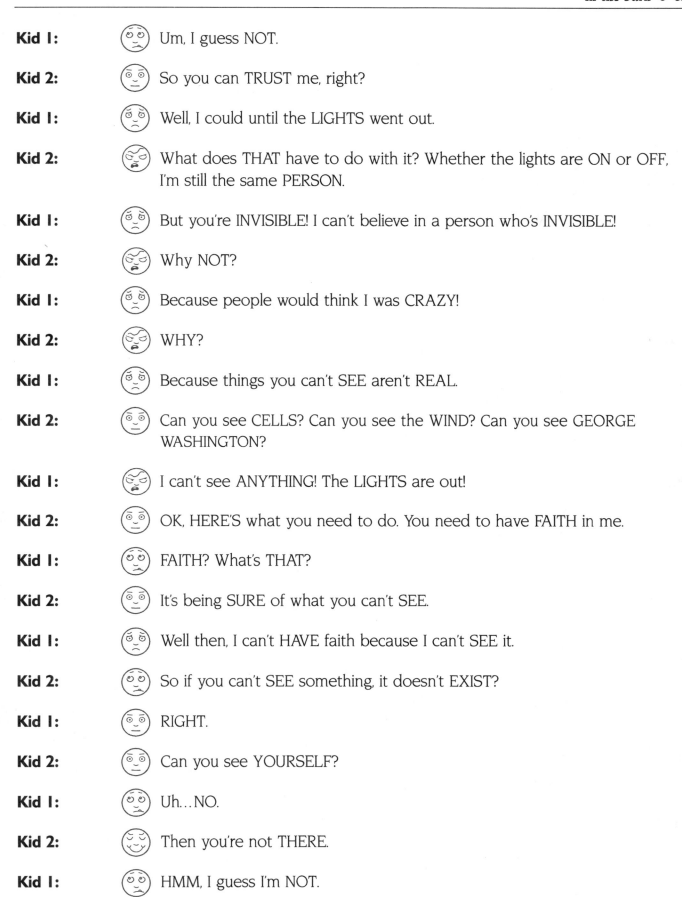

Kid 2: 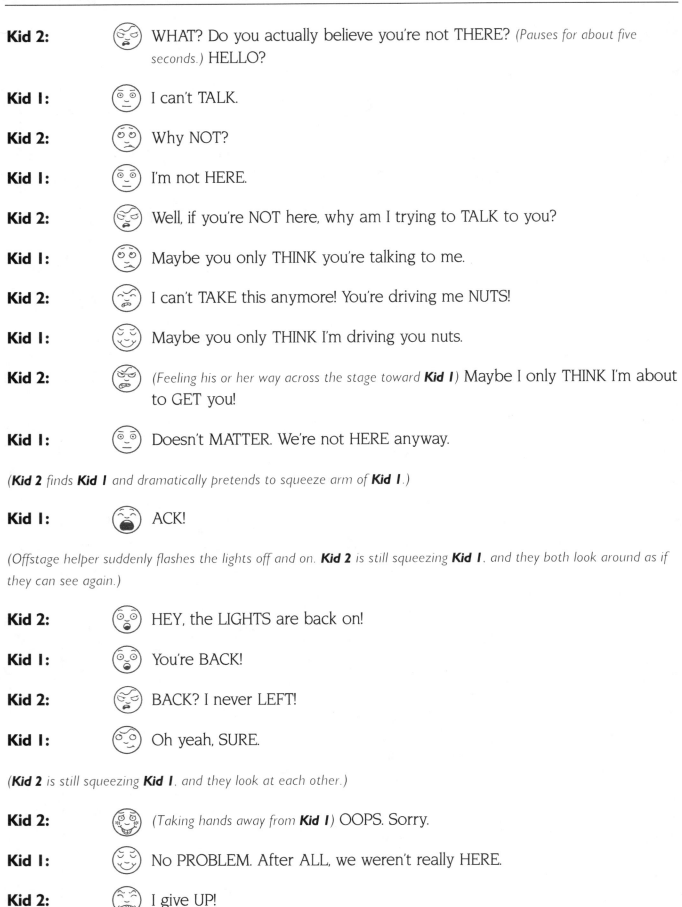 WHAT? Do you actually believe you're not THERE? *(Pauses for about five seconds.)* HELLO?

Kid 1: I can't TALK.

Kid 2: Why NOT?

Kid 1: I'm not HERE.

Kid 2: Well, if you're NOT here, why am I trying to TALK to you?

Kid 1: Maybe you only THINK you're talking to me.

Kid 2: I can't TAKE this anymore! You're driving me NUTS!

Kid 1: Maybe you only THINK I'm driving you nuts.

Kid 2: *(Feeling his or her way across the stage toward **Kid 1**)* Maybe I only THINK I'm about to GET you!

Kid 1: Doesn't MATTER. We're not HERE anyway.

*(**Kid 2** finds **Kid 1** and dramatically pretends to squeeze arm of **Kid 1**.)*

Kid 1: ACK!

*(Offstage helper suddenly flashes the lights off and on. **Kid 2** is still squeezing **Kid 1**, and they both look around as if they can see again.)*

Kid 2: HEY, the LIGHTS are back on!

Kid 1: You're BACK!

Kid 2: BACK? I never LEFT!

Kid 1: Oh yeah, SURE.

*(**Kid 2** is still squeezing **Kid 1**, and they look at each other.)*

Kid 2: *(Taking hands away from **Kid 1**)* OOPS. Sorry.

Kid 1: No PROBLEM. After ALL, we weren't really HERE.

Kid 2: I give UP!

Kid 1: GOOD. Let's decorate the GYM.

Kid 2: NAH, that would take all NIGHT. I've got a BETTER idea.

Kid 1: WHAT?

Kid 2: We just TURN OUT THE LIGHTS. Then the gym won't EXIST anymore. No GYM, no PARTY!

Kid 1: But...

Kid 2: *(Interrupting)* TRUST me. NOBODY will MIND.

*(**Kid 2** starts leading **Kid 1** toward the stage exit.)*

Kid 1: But...

Kid 2: *(Interrupting)* Don't WORRY. Remember, SEEING is BELIEVING—right?

Kid 1: But...

Kid 2: *(Interrupting)* This will be the BEST VALENTINE'S DAY EVER!

Kid 1: I'll BELIEVE it...when I SEE it!

*(**Kids 1** and **2** exit the stage.)*

● **To Talk About:**

- How is believing in God like believing that a friend is there during a blackout? How is it different?
- When we have doubts about God, how do you think God reacts? Explain.
- When is it most difficult for you to believe that God is there? when you've done something wrong, when your prayers seem to go unanswered, when someone laughs at your beliefs
- When have you felt most sure that God was there? How do you feel when you re-member that time?

● **Other Topical Tie-Ins:**

Doubt   God's existence   When God seems far away

It's Only Words

Topic: Prayer

Scriptures You Might Read: Matthew 6:5-13; James 5:13-16

The Scene: A home and a school

The Simple Setup: You'll need to place a table and two chairs slightly to the right or left of center stage. **Teacher** should dress as a teacher; the other actors may wear casual clothes. Make sure **Audrey** understands what a singsong voice is; let her practice her lines if at all possible.

Puppet Options: You could use puppets for all the roles. If you'd like to include a leader, cast him or her as **Narrator**. If you use puppets, you won't need a table and chairs.

Extra Touches: If you have a keyboard player who can improvise, ask him or her to add musical transitions—for example, happy music at the skit's beginning, otherworldly sounds as **Audrey** sleeps, and a sad tune when **Audrey** alienates Friend.

The Characters:
> **Narrator,** a friendly storyteller
> **Audrey,** a girl who loves to talk (except to God)
> **Friend,** her classmate
> **Brother,** her sibling
> **Teacher,** her favorite instructor

*(As the skit begins, the stage is empty, except for the furniture. **Narrator** may be offstage or at one side of the stage throughout the skit.)*

Narrator: ONCE upon a TIME, there was a GIRL named AUDREY.

*(**Audrey** enters the stage, stands, and smiles.)*

Narrator: Of ALL the things there were to DO in the world, Audrey MOST liked to TALK. She talked to her FRIENDS…

*(**Friend** enters the stage and approaches **Audrey**, smiling.)*

Audrey: *(Speaking with lots of energy)* HI! Did you see that show about LIZARDS last night? I sure had a lot of HOMEWORK. How about those awful CORN DOGS at LUNCH today? HEY, after SCHOOL let's see if our MOMS will take us SKATING. BYE!

(**Friend** smiles, waves, and exits the stage.)

Narrator: She talked to her FAMILY...

(**Brother** enters the stage and approaches **Audrey**, smiling.)

Audrey: (Speaking with lots of energy) HI, brother! CONGRATULATIONS on WINNING the TRACK MEET! Do you think MOM will let us get a PUPPY? You sure cleaned your room FAST yesterday. HEY, after DINNER let's make some POPCORN and play a GAME. BYE!

(**Brother** smiles, waves, and exits the stage.)

Narrator: She talked to her TEACHER...

(**Teacher** enters the stage and approaches **Audrey**, smiling.)

Audrey: (Speaking with lots of energy) HI, Mrs. Appleby! You sure look NICE today! Thanks for helping me figure out how to write that PAPER last week. Do you mind if I do my BOOK REPORT on *WHERE'S WALDO?* instead of *MOBY DICK*? HEY, can I get EXTRA CREDIT if I go on a FIELD TRIP to the MOON? BYE!

(**Teacher** smiles, waves, and exits the stage.)

Narrator: And SOMETIMES Audrey even talked to GOD. But when she DID, it WAS...DIFFERENT.

Audrey: (Bowing her head and talking in a singsong voice) LORD, we THANK you for this FOOD. It is very, very GOOD. (Yawns.) NOW I lay me DOWN to SLEEP. I PRAY the Lord my SOUL to KEEP. If I should die before I WAKE, I pray the Lord my SOUL to TAKE. (Yawns again.) AMEN. (Nods off to sleep and snores.)

Narrator: ONE NIGHT after Audrey had PRAYED the SAME PRAYER for the FIFTEEN-HUNDREDTH TIME, she fell ASLEEP. And WHILE she slept, something HAPPENED. In the MORNING when she woke UP, things had...CHANGED.

(**Audrey** stretches and opens her eyes. She walks to the table and sits on a chair. **Brother** enters the stage, stretching, and sits on the other chair.)

Brother: YO, sis. What's HAPPENIN'?

Audrey: *(Speaking in a singsong voice)* PASS the PANCAKES if you PLEASE, ORANGE juice, and EGGS with CHEESE. *(Yawns.)* CEREAL is GOOD to EAT; TOAST and JAM are such a TREAT. *(Yawns, then frowns as if trying to figure out why she's talking so strangely.)*

Brother: How come you're talking so WEIRD? It's like you're just saying WORDS— like you're not really TALKING to ME. Like I'm not even HERE. So in about THREE SECONDS, I WON'T be!

*(**Brother** exits the stage. **Audrey** gets up, looking puzzled, and slowly walks toward center stage.)*

Narrator: *What is going ON?* Audrey wondered. She went to SCHOOL, hoping to find OUT.

*(**Friend** enters the stage and approaches **Audrey**.)*

Friend: HI, Audrey! How's it…

Audrey: *(Interrupting and speaking in a singsong voice)* GIMME THIS and GIMME THAT; if you DON'T, you're just a BRAT. *(Yawns.)*

Friend: WHAT?

Audrey: *(Speaking in a singsong voice)* Being FRIENDS is not ENOUGH; GIMME, GIMME, GIMME stuff. *(Yawns.)*

Friend: GIVE you stuff? I want to be your FRIEND, not your SLAVE! If you only like me for what you can GET, I don't think I want to spend TIME with you!

*(**Friend** exits the stage. **Audrey** opens her mouth as if she wants to say something, but nothing comes out.)*

Narrator: When CLASS began, Audrey tried talking to her TEACHER.

*(**Teacher** enters the stage and approaches **Audrey**.)*

Teacher: HELLO, Audrey. What can I…

Audrey: *(Interrupting and speaking in a singsong voice)* I didn't STUDY for the TEST, but FIX IT so my GRADE is BEST. *(Yawns.)*

Teacher: I BEG your PARDON?

Audrey: *(Speaking in a singsong voice)* TALKING to you is such a BORE; I'm SURE it's my LEAST FAVORITE CHORE. *(Yawns.)*

Teacher: YOUNG LADY, you must have FORGOTTEN who you're TALKING to. Since you don't wish to show PROPER RESPECT, I'm sending you out in the HALL to THINK about it.

*(**Teacher** exits the stage. **Audrey** sadly walks a few steps, then stands as if in the hall.)*

Narrator: Audrey stood in the HALL, THINKING. WHAT was the MATTER with her? It was almost as if she were talking to her FRIENDS, FAMILY, and TEACHERS the SAME WAY she usually talked to...GOD.

Audrey: UH-oh.

Narrator: Audrey decided to PRAY about it.

Audrey: *(Bows her head.)* LORD, we THANK you for this FOOD... No, no, WAIT. NOW I lay me DOWN to SLEEP... AARGH! I've got to STOP JUST SAYING WORDS and really TALK! Dear GOD, I'm SORRY I've only said a bunch of WORDS instead of really TALKING to you. I've treated you in ways I wouldn't treat my FRIENDS or FAMILY or TEACHERS. Please help me remember that you're really HERE, that I need to talk about MORE than what I want, and that I need to show RESPECT to you. AMEN. *(Looks up.)* HEY! I talked without RHYMES! And I didn't sound like I was falling ASLEEP! I'm CURED!

Narrator: And THAT'S how Audrey learned to TALK...to EVERYBODY.

Audrey: *(Speaking as she walks toward exit.)* HEY, everybody! Let's TALK! *(Exits the stage.)*

Narrator: And they talked HAPPILY ever AFTER.

● **To Talk About:**
- How is talking to God like talking to a friend? How is it different?
- What was one of the shortest prayers you ever prayed? What was one of the longest? Why weren't they the same?
- If you could see God, would it change the way you talk to him? If so, how?
- How do you think God feels about the way you talk to him? Why?

● **Other Topical Tie-Ins:**

Having a relationship with God   Believing that God is there   Breaking bad habits

Knights of the Square Table

Topic: Prejudice

Scriptures You Might Read: Romans 12:3, 16; James 2:1-9

The Scene: A meeting place

The Simple Setup: You'll need four chairs and a card table (or another square table) with a pencil and paper on it. All actors may wear casual clothes, and actors of either gender could play all roles, with minor word changes.

Puppet Options: You could use puppets for all the roles, or you could use a mixture of puppets and real actors. You won't need chairs for the puppets, of course.

Extra Touches: If you'd like, make a club logo for the Knights of the Square Table—a picture of crossed swords on a square, for instance—and hang it on the wall behind the table.

The Characters:
    Kid 1, an organized snob
    Kid 2, an excitable snob
    Kid 3, a cranky snob
    Kid 4, an extra-snobbish snob

(As the skit begins, all the characters are seated at the table.)

Kid 1: OK, this meeting of our NEW CLUB, the KNIGHTS OF THE SQUARE TABLE, is CALLED TO ORDER. The SECRETARY will READ THE MINUTES from the LAST meeting.

Kid 2: There WASN'T any last meeting. This is the FIRST meeting we've ever HAD.

Kid 1: Oh, RIGHT. Well, any NEW BUSINESS?

Kid 3: YEAH. We need to decide who CAN'T be in our CLUB. What kind of club would it BE if just ANYBODY could be in it?

Kid 4: Especially THOSE people.

Kid 3: YEAH!—THOSE people.

Kid 1:   OK. All in favor of keeping THOSE people out of our club, RAISE your HANDS.

(All characters raise their hands.)

Kid 1:   That SETTLES it. From now ON, THOSE people will NOT be allowed to join the KNIGHTS OF THE SQUARE TABLE. Now is there any OTHER new...

Kid 2:   *(Interrupting)* Uh, maybe we should WRITE DOWN exactly who THOSE people are. Just so there isn't any CONFUSION.

Kid 4:   Hey, I'M not confused! EVERYBODY knows who THOSE people are.

Kid 1:   Of COURSE everybody knows. But let's write it down ANYWAY. It'll just take a MINUTE. *(Picks up a pencil and writes on paper, reading aloud while writing.)* OK. "THOSE PEOPLE...are ANYONE who...DOESN'T LIKE ICE SKATING...PUTS KETCHUP ON SCRAMBLED EGGS...or HAS A PET FISH AT HOME."

Kid 2:   Hey, WAIT a minute! I'VE got a pet fish at home!

Kid 1:   WELL, then, I guess you must be one of THOSE people.

Kid 2:   I am NOT! *(Takes the paper and pencil. Reads aloud while writing.)* "THOSE people are ANYONE WHO LIKES COUNTRY MUSIC...CAN'T RIDE A BIKE WITHOUT TRAINING WHEELS...or HASN'T LIVED IN THIS TOWN AS LONG AS I HAVE."

Kid 3:   Hold ON! I LIKE country music!

Kid 2:   Well, I guess you must be one of THOSE people.

Kid 3:   No WAY! *(Takes the paper and pencil. Reads aloud while writing.)* "THOSE people are ANYONE WHO KNOWS HOW TO COUNT TO TEN IN FRENCH...HAS MORE FRECKLES THAN I DO...or HAS A HOUSE WITH ONLY ONE BATHROOM."

Kid 4:   WHOA! MY house has only one bathroom!

Kid 3:   OOH! One of THOSE people, eh?

Kid 4:   Don't CALL me that! *(Takes the paper and pencil. Reads aloud while writing.)* EVERYBODY knows "THOSE people are ANYONE WHO'S LEFT-HANDED...PLAYS VOLLEYBALL...or WEARS MORE EXPENSIVE JEANS THAN I DO."

Kid 1:   Hey, I'M a volleyball player!

Kid 4:   Well, I guess YOU know what YOU are!

(All the characters start arguing with each other, saying, "You're one of THOSE people" and "I know YOU are, but what am I?" and other similar phrases.)

Kid 1:   STOP! Quiet DOWN! There's only ONE thing to do. We all voted to keep THOSE people out of the club, so we'll ALL have to leave.

Kid 2:   ALL of us?

Kid 3:   But then there won't BE any club. Each of us will be totally ALONE!

*(**Kids 2, 3,** and **4** frown, thinking. Then they all smile.)*

Kids 2, 3, and 4:   *(Speaking together)* What a GREAT IDEA!

Kid 2:   So LONG! I'm going to start my OWN club! *(Exits the stage.)*

Kid 3:   Me TOO! Who wants to waste time with YOU? *(Exits the stage.)*

Kid 4:   Boy, THAT was a close one! I almost had to spend time with... THOSE people! *(Exits the stage.)*

Kid 1:   *(Looks around to make sure everyone else is gone.)* Hey, it WORKED! I've got the whole club to MYSELF! Boy, this is gonna be a GREAT club. First I'll... Well, NO, that takes TOO MANY PEOPLE But I can...OH. I'd need MORE PEOPLE for that. *(Sags in chair and looks around at empty chairs.)* Yeah, I'm having SOME FUN NOW. *(Pauses, then suddenly stands up.)* HEY, everyone! Wait for ME! *(Exits the stage.)*

● To Talk About:

- Why did the characters all mean something different when they talked about "those people"? If people at your school talked about "those people," who might they mean?
- Has anyone ever seemed prejudiced toward you? If so, how did you feel?
- Using our own words, how could we turn James 2:1-9 into guidelines for keeping prejudice out of this group?

● Other Topical Tie-Ins:

Accepting one another   Pride   Welcoming newcomers

The Lyin' King

Topic: Telling the Truth

Scriptures You Might Read: Psalm 15; Proverbs 12:22

The Scene: A clearing in the jungle

The Simple Setup: Place a chair in the middle of the stage. **Kid** will need a small bag and a piece of paper. **Kid** could wear a pith helmet if one is available. **Hunter** should carry a toy rifle and, if possible, wear a hunter's outfit (safari gear or camouflage clothes). The other actors may wear casual clothing. Have an offstage helper provide the "thud" or "cracking branch" sound. (Note: You might want to go over the pronunciation of "hakuna matata"—huh-KOO-nuh muh-TAH-tuh—especially if the actor playing **Kid** hasn't seen *The Lion King*. You may want to go over the pronunciation of *sayonara* as well.)

Puppet Options: Using puppets would allow you to cast a lion in the role of the **Lyin' King** and even **Kid**, if you like. Or all puppets could be people puppets. If you want to mix puppets and live actors, cast a child as **Kid** or a leader as **Hunter**.

Extra Touches: If possible, play music from the soundtrack of the animated film, *The Lion King*, at the beginning and end of the skit. The song, "Circle of Life," would be especially appropriate at the end.

The Characters:
> **The Lyin' King**, a not-so-smooth-talking liar
> **Kid**, an eager but misguided student
> **Hunter**, a tough but fair pursuer

*(As the skit begins, the **Lyin' King** is sitting in a chair and stretching lazily. After a few moments, **Kid** enters the stage as if making his way through jungle vines. Finally he sees the **Lyin' King**.)*

Kid:	😕	EXCUSE me, have you seen the one called THE LYIN' KING?
King:	😌	The LYIN' KING? The one who's better at LYIN' than anyone else in the JUNGLE? THAT Lyin' King?
Kid:	😃	YES!
King:	😌	NOPE. Never HEARD of him.
Kid:	🙁	But I've got to FIND him. I've traveled for WEEKS through this jungle,

swimming RIVERS, climbing MOUNTAINS, wrestling CROCODILES...

King: *(Trying to interrupt)* I...

Kid: ...fighting SNAKES, killing SPIDERS, punching ARMADILLOS...

King: *(Interrupting)* All RIGHT, already! I get the PICTURE!

Kid: ...all to find the famous LYIN' KING.

King: And why do you want to FIND this Lyin' King?

Kid: So he can teach ME to be a GREAT LIAR, TOO.

King: HMM. And what does the Lyin' King GET in RETURN?

Kid: MONEY! I brought all my MONEY with me.

King: Oh, THAT Lyin' King! Yeah, I saw him just TEN MINUTES AGO. *(Pointing offstage)* He went THAT WAY!

Kid: THANK you! *(Starts to leave.)*

King: HA! GOTCHA!

Kid: HUH?

King: It's ME, kid! I'm the guy you're LOOKING for! I'm THE LYIN' KING!

Kid: WOW! You ARE a good liar!

King: NO, I'm not.

Kid: WHAT?

King: Gotcha AGAIN!

Kid: Oh, Lyin' King, can you teach ME how to be a great liar TOO?

King SURE, kid. But FIRST, show me the MONEY!

Kid: *(Holding up the bag)* HERE!

King: OK! HOW TO BE A GREAT LIAR, LESSON NUMBER ONE. Always remember: HAKUNA POTATO!

Kid: What does THAT mean?

King: It means...uh..."NO PROBLEM." No matter how many LIES you tell, they'll NEVER cause any PROBLEMS.

Kid: REALLY?

King: TRUST me, kid. I've been lyin' for YEARS, and nothing's ever... *(Pauses.)* HEY, did you HEAR something?

Kid: Nope. So, what's lesson number TWO?

King: Uh...HAKUNA...TOMATO.

Kid: What's THAT mean?

King: It means...um..."NO PUNISHMENT." No matter how many LIES you tell, you'll NEVER be PUNISHED.

Kid: Are you SURE?

King: HEY, kid, would I LIE to you? *(Pauses.)* HMM, did you HEAR something?

Kid: I don't THINK so. What's lesson number THREE?

King: Well, it's...

(Offstage helper makes a thud sound or the sound of cracking of branches.)

King: Uh...did you HEAR something?

Kid: DEFINITELY.

King: That's what I THOUGHT. I gotta RUN, kid!

Kid: But WAIT! You didn't tell me lesson number THREE!

King: Uh...HAKUNA...SAYONARA!

Kid: What does THAT mean?

King: It means "NO TIME TO EXPLAIN!" BYE, kid, and THANKS for the MONEY! *(Grabs bag and runs off the stage.)*

Kid: HEY! Come BACK!

*(**Hunter** enters the stage.)*

Hunter: Excuse me, have you seen the one they call the LYIN' KING?

Kid: Um…er…NO.

Hunter: You're not a very good LIAR, ARE you?

Kid: I only got to lesson TWO.

Hunter: So you HAVE seen the Lyin' King.

Kid: YEAH. But why are you HUNTING for him?

Hunter: Because of THE CIRCLE OF LIES.

Kid: The CIRCLE OF LIES? What's THAT?

Hunter: When you tell a LIE, it comes back to HAUNT you. It may take a long TIME, but eventually it CATCHES up. It's like a big CIRCLE—the CIRCLE OF LIES.

Kid: But the LYIN' KING said lies NEVER catch up with you! NO PROBLEMS! NO PUNISHMENT!

Hunter: That's why they call him the LYIN' KING.

Kid: Oh. RIGHT.

Hunter: Well, it's time for me to CATCH UP with him. GOODBYE. And REMEMBER… HAKUNA MATATA!

Kid: What does THAT mean?

Hunter: It means "NO WORRIES." If you REALLY want to have NO WORRIES, always TELL THE TRUTH. *(Exits the stage.)*

Kid: I guess he's RIGHT. Well, I'd better get MOVING. *(Takes a piece of paper from pocket.)* I've got to start taking those VINE-SWINGING LESSONS from this OTHER guy… *(looking at paper)* GEORGE of the JUNGLE. *(Exits the stage.)*

● **To Talk About:**

- Is there really such a thing as a "great liar"? Why or why not?
- Do you agree that if you want to have no worries, you should tell the truth? Why or why not?
- What "price" might the following kids have to pay for their lies?
    - a girl who spreads the untrue rumor that her friend painted graffiti on the school
    - a boy who denies stealing the gym teacher's stopwatch, even though he did
    - a girl who tells her parents she isn't taking drugs, even though she is
- If for seven days, no one in the world could tell a lie, how might life at your school or home change by the end of the week?

● **Other Topical Tie-Ins:**

The results of sin   Setting good goals   Worry

Someone Who Has Everything

Topic: What God Is Like

Scriptures You Might Read: Psalm 29; 1 John 3:1-3

The Scene: A store

The Simple Setup: No set or props are required. **Salesperson** should be dressed up; other actors may wear casual clothes. Actors of either gender could play all roles, with minor word changes.

Puppet Options: You could use puppets for all the roles. If you want to mix puppets and live actors, cast a leader as **Salesperson** or a child as **Kid**.

Extra Touches: To help identify the setting, you might want to add a toy cash register, a couple of "sale" signs, or a table of "merchandise."

The Characters:
    Salesperson, a know-it-all
    Kid, a friendly but earnest would-be customer
    Shopper, an average customer

*(As the skit begins, **Kid** is looking around. **Salesperson** walks up to **Kid**.)*

Salesperson: Welcome to PRESENTS R US! May I HELP you?

Kid: I THINK so. Do you sell PRESENTS here?

Salesperson: Of COURSE! Why do you think we call it PRESENTS R US?

Kid: Oh. SORRY.

Salesperson: THAT'S all right. REMEMBER, there are NO STUPID QUESTIONS—just DUMB ones. Now what KIND of present are you LOOKING for?

Kid: Well, I don't KNOW exactly.

Salesperson: Say no MORE! You've come to the RIGHT PLACE. I am not just a SALESPERSON, you know. I am a HIGHLY TRAINED PRESENT EXPERT.

Kid: What's THAT?

Salesperson: It means that if you TELL me about the PERSON you're buying the PRESENT for, I can tell you WHAT TO GET.

Kid: WOW!

Salesperson: NOW how OLD is this someone?

Kid: Uh, I don't KNOW.

Salesperson: Well, ABOUT how old? TWO? TEN? TWENTY? A HUNDRED and SIX?

Kid: Oh, WAY more than THAT. He's been around, like, FOREVER.

Salesperson: I SEE. Well, let's just say he's…GROWN-UP.

Kid: RIGHT.

Salesperson: And what are this someone's HOBBIES?

Kid: HOBBIES?

Salesperson: YES. What does he like to DO?

Kid: Um, he likes…to MAKE things.

Salesperson: Such AS?

Kid: Oh, MOUNTAINS…RIVERS…ANIMALS…

Salesperson: So he's an ARTIST?

Kid: SORT of, but…

Salesperson: (Interrupting) We'll just say he's into CRAFTS.

Kid: But…

Salesperson: (Interrupting) Don't WORRY! I'm a HIGHLY TRAINED PRESENT EXPERT. I KNOW what I'm DOING.

Kid: OK.

Salesperson: Now, let's say you decided to give this someone some CLOTHES as a present. Do you know his SIZE?

Kid: Oh, HUGE!

Salesperson: HOW huge?

Kid: Well, he can be EVERYWHERE AT ONCE if he WANTS to. So I guess you could say he's as HUGE as the UNIVERSE.

Salesperson: HMM. He would need something from our BIG AND TALL DEPARTMENT then.

Kid: At LEAST!

Salesperson: ONE more QUESTION. How would you describe his PERSONALITY? Is this someone QUIET or LOUD?

Kid: YES.

Salesperson: GENTLE or POWERFUL?

Kid: YES.

Salesperson: SERIOUS, or have a sense of HUMOR?

Kid: YES.

Salesperson: Now WAIT a minute! You're supposed to CHOOSE ONE or the OTHER! He can't be ALL those things!

Kid: But this someone IS. And he's also LOVING, FORGIVING, and PERFECT.

Salesperson: But NOBODY'S PERFECT! Nobody except…

Kid: GOD.

Salesperson: WHAT? You want to give a present to GOD?

Kid: SURE!

Salesperson: WHY? Is it his BIRTHDAY?

Kid: NO! God's been around FOREVER, remember? I want to give God a present because he's DONE SO MUCH for ME.

Salesperson: What can you possibly give to GOD?

Kid: I don't KNOW. YOU'RE the HIGHLY TRAINED PRESENT EXPERT.

Salesperson: OH, that's RIGHT. *(Composing himself/herself.)* Very WELL. Why don't you give God...some MONEY?

Kid: God already OWNS all the money.

Salesperson: How about...a nice GIFT BOX of SAUSAGES AND CHEESE?

Kid: God already OWNS all the FOOD.

Salesperson: A MANSION with SEVEN HUNDRED ROOMS and TWELVE SWIMMING POOLS?

Kid: OWNS it.

Salesperson: The state of ALASKA?

Kid: OWNS it.

Salesperson: The WORLD?

Kid: OWNS it.

Salesperson: I give UP! There IS no present for the SOMEONE WHO HAS EVERYTHING!

Kid: But the SIGN on your STORE says, "PRESENTS FOR THE SOMEONE WHO HAS EVERYTHING."

Salesperson: We just said that because it SOUNDED good!

Kid: There MUST be SOMETHING I can give to God. Something God can't USE the way he WANTS to until I decide to GIVE it to him. *(Pauses.)* HEY, I know! I could give God my HEART!

Salesperson: Your HEART? YUCK!

Kid: NO, NO. I mean MYSELF. The REAL me. The part that CHOOSES WHAT TO DO, who to FOLLOW.

Salesperson: Oh.

Kid: Now I just need to figure out HOW to give myself to God.

Salesperson: Try our GIFT WRAP DEPARTMENT—second floor, near the elevator.

Kid: OK, THANKS! *(Exits the stage.)*

Shopper: *(Enters the stage and approaches **Salesperson**.)* HI! I'm looking for a PRESENT.

Salesperson: Is it for a HUGE, LOVING, GENTLE, POWERFUL, PERFECT SOMEONE WHO'S BEEN AROUND FOREVER AND ALREADY OWNS EVERYTHING?

Shopper: Why, YES! How did you KNOW?

Salesperson: *(Speaking to the audience)* I need a VACATION. *(Exits the stage.)*

*(After a pause, **Shopper** shrugs and exits.)*

● **To Talk About:**
- How would you describe to a three-year-old what God is like?
- Which of these is most important to you right now: God's power, love, sense of humor, or ownership of everything? Why?
- What are some of the "presents" God has given you?
- Have you ever tried to do something for God?
- Instead of wrapping ourselves in gift wrap, how can we give ourselves to God?

● **Other Topical Tie-Ins:**

God's power   Giving ourselves to God   Thanksgiving

The Miracle Worker

Topic: God's Power

Scriptures You Might Read: Matthew 12:38-39; 25:34-40

The Scene: A bedroom

The Simple Setup: No set or props are required, though you may want to place a chair at center stage for **Jesse** to kneel at. All actors may wear casual clothes. Have an offstage helper provide the knocking sound. Actors of either gender could play the roles of **Jesse, Kid 1,** and **Kid 2,** with minor word changes. Let **Jesse** know that he or she may pray with eyes open to read the script.

Puppet Options: You could use puppets for all the roles. Or you could use a puppet as **Jesse** and have children and leaders fill the other roles.

Extra Touches: To help establish the setting, you could place a bed at center stage and have **Jesse** kneel next to it.

The Characters:
    Jesse, who has many demands
    Man, a helpful neighbor
    Kid 1, a friend of Jesse's
    Mom, Jesse's mother
    Kid 2, a door-to-door fund-raiser

(As the skit begins, **Jesse** *enters the stage and walks to the center of the stage.)*

Jesse: OK, TIME to PRAY. *(Kneels.)* DEAR GOD, it's ME, JESSE. You've been hearing from me all WEEK, REMEMBER? I keep asking you to DO these things, but nothing HAPPENS! It's as if you're not even LISTENING. For instance, on MONDAY I asked you for a NEW BIKE. Now, I KNOW I already HAVE a bike, but it's got a FLAT TIRE and a big SCRATCH on the paint. So I thought you could do a MIRACLE and one morning I'd open the DOOR and find a BRAND NEW BIKE. But NO! Every DAY this week, I've opened the DOOR, and...NOTHING. Now how am I supposed to ride to... *(Offstage helper interrupts with a knocking sound.)* Man, who's THAT? *(Gets up.)* Come IN!

Man: *(Entering the stage)* HI, Jesse! Since I live right down the STREET, I couldn't help noticing you were having TROUBLE with your BIKE. So I FIXED the FLAT TIRE and PAINTED OVER that SCRATCH. Have a GOOD DAY, OK? *(Exits the stage.)*

Jesse: How can I have a GOOD DAY when I don't have a NEW BIKE? *(Kneels again.)* Now where WAS I? Oh, YEAH. Why haven't you done a MIRACLE? Can't you HEAR me? HELLO? Would it be so HARD to make a BRIGHT, SHINY, NEW RED BIKE appear on my DOORSTEP? I mean, you PARTED the RED SEA, RIGHT? Wasn't that more DIFFICULT? *(Pauses.)* Well, I can see that you're not going to DO anything about the BIKE. The NEXT item on my list was the big MATH TEST coming up. I just can't get those TIMES TABLES! So I asked you to do a MIRACLE and POUR all those ANSWERS right into my BRAIN. But you DIDN'T! The test is TOMORROW, and I STILL haven't learned that stuff. I even SLEPT with my MATH BOOK under my PILLOW, but nothing HAPPENED! Don't you CARE whether I PASS the TEST? Don't you... *(Offstage helper interrupts with a knocking sound.)* What is it NOW? *(Stands up.)* Can't a person get any PRAYING done around here? Come IN!

Kid 1: *(Enters the stage.)* HEY, Jesse! Sine we're both in the same MATH CLASS, I was wondering if you'd like to STUDY together for the BIG TEST. You could help me learn FRACTIONS, and I could help you learn the TIMES TABLES.

Jesse: STUDY? I haven't got time to STUDY! Can't you see that I'm PRAYING here?

Kid 1: Oh, SORRY. Well, I hope you do OK on the TEST tomorrow. BYE! *(Exits the stage.)*

Jesse: *(Kneeling again)* THAT was pretty rude, BARGING IN while I'm trying to PRAY! So ANYWAY, God, you're obviously not going to DO anything about my MATH PROBLEM. I thought you could do MIRACLES. I thought you were POWERFUL. But I guess NOT, huh? If you WERE, you would have DONE something about the NEXT item on my list. Yeah, I'm talking about the CAVITY in my TOOTH! It HURTS whenever I CHEW. I asked you for a LITTLE, TINY MIRACLE—YOU know, SNAP YOUR FINGERS and MAKE IT BETTER—but it STILL HURTS! I thought you could HEAL people! I thought you could do ANYTHING! I thought... *(Offstage helper interrupts with a knocking sound.)* I can't BELIEVE this! *(Stands up.)* Why won't people leave me ALONE? Come IN, already!

Mom: *(Enters the stage.)* JESSE?

Jesse: YEAH, Mom, what IS it?

Mom: I just talked to the DENTIST, and he can FIX your TOOTH on WEDNESDAY. Isn't that GREAT? See you LATER! *(Exits the stage.)*

Jesse: NO, that's NOT great! It's TERRIBLE! I don't want to go to the DENTIST! *(Kneels again.)* I guess you're not as strong as people SAY, huh, Lord? Otherwise you would have HEALED my TOOTH. Or maybe you just don't CARE. Yeah, THAT'S it. THAT explains why you didn't do that LAST miracle on my list. It wasn't even for ME! It was for those STARVING PEOPLE! All I wanted was for you to FEED them, maybe split up some BREAD AND FISH like you did that time in the BIBLE… *(Offstage helper interrupts with a knocking sound.)* This is getting RIDICULOUS! *(Stands up.)* All RIGHT, come IN!

Kid 2: HI, I'm raising MONEY to FEED STARVING PEOPLE. Would you like to HELP? Any amount you can GIVE would be WONDERFUL.

Jesse: WHAT? ME give MONEY? If I give you MONEY, how will I SAVE UP for a NEW BIKE?

Kid 2: I just SAW your bike OUTSIDE. It looked OK to ME.

Jesse: OUT! Get OUT!

*(**Kid 2** exits the stage.)*

Jesse: *(**Jesse** looks up, as if to heaven.)* Just a FEW LITTLE MIRACLES—that's all I WANTED! But NO! It's OBVIOUS that you've got a PROBLEM. You know what it IS? You're just not paying ATTENTION! *(Exits the stage.)*

● **To Talk About:**
- Who wasn't paying attention in this skit? Explain.
- How did God respond to Jesse's request for a new bike? help with math? a healed tooth? food for starving people?
- What do you think a miracle is? Have you ever seen one? Were there any in this skit? Explain.
- How might you be the answer to someone else's prayer for a miracle this week?

● **Other Topical Tie-Ins:**

Prayer   Miracles   Serving others

No One's Ark

Topic: Following God's Instructions

Scriptures You Might Read: Genesis 6–8; Psalm 119:97-104

The Scene: A gathering place in biblical times

The Simple Setup: No set is required. **Noah** will need a small toy boat as a prop. Station **Crowd Members 1, 2,** and **3** in the audience; they and **Noah** should wear robes and headgear that suggest Bible-times clothing.

Puppet Options: You could use puppets for all the roles. Use any adult male Bible-times puppet for **Noah** and any male or female Bible-times puppets for **Crowd Members**. If you use this option, place **Crowd Members** onstage rather than in the audience (unless you have more than one stage). Or use a puppet only for **Noah**, and cast leaders or children as **Crowd Members** and station them in the audience. Note that if **Noah** is a puppet, he'll need to produce the toy boat from behind the puppet stage rather than from his pocket.

Extra Touches: If you'd like, add thunder sound effects toward the end of the skit when the characters realize it's starting to rain. Use audiocassettes or have an offstage helper shake some sheet metal.

The Characters:
    Noah, a nervous ark builder
    Crowd Member 1, who's a bit hard of hearing
    Crowd Member 2, who's a bit curious
    Crowd Member 3, who's a bit confused

*(As the skit begins, **Crowd Members** are stationed in the audience. **Noah** enters, looking nervously at the audience. Finally he works up the courage to speak.)*

Noah: Uh, HI! Nice to see…so many of you HERE. Uh, as MOST of you KNOW, my name is NOAH…

Crowd Member 1: *(Interrupting)* Speak UP, would you? Some of us can't HEAR you in the BACK!

Noah: Oh, SORRY. *(Speaking louder)* My name is NOAH, and I suppose you're WONDERING why I CALLED you all here today.

Crowd Member 2: Is it about the BOAT?

Noah: Uh, the BOAT. Well, YES. But I'll get to that in a MINUTE.

Crowd Member 3: Is it time to get IN the BOAT?

Noah: Er, not EXACTLY. I'll get to THAT in just…

Crowd Member 1: *(Interrupting)* Could you speak UP? All these PAIRS of ANIMALS back here are REALLY NOISY!

Noah: OK! *(Clears throat.)* Well, a while back I got a MESSAGE from GOD. He wanted me to BUILD an ARK.

Crowd Member 2: I thought it was a BOAT.

Noah: YES. An ark is a KIND of boat.

Crowd Member 2: Oh.

Noah: Now God wanted me to BUILD this ark because he's planning to send a FLOOD to COVER THE EARTH. He gave me INSTRUCTIONS on how to BUILD the ark. He said to make it 450 FEET LONG, 75 FEET WIDE, and 45 FEET HIGH.

Crowd Member 2: WOW! That's a BIG BOAT!

Noah: Um, YES. Yes, it IS.

Crowd Member 3: SO is it time to get in the BOAT yet?

Noah Uh, NO, but I'll GET to that. ANYWAY, I started BUILDING the ark, but I was afraid people would LAUGH at me and think I was CRAZY. So I decided to build the ark where people couldn't SEE it—in my BACKYARD.

Crowd Member 2: But how could such a BIG BOAT fit in your BACKYARD?

Noah: Um, it COULDN'T. So I...I decided to make the ark a little SMALLER.

Crowd Member 2: HOW small?

Noah: Fifty feet.

Crowd Member 1: Could you SPEAK UP? These ELEPHANTS back here are awfully LOUD!

Noah: FIFTY FEET! I decided to make it FIFTY FEET LONG!

Crowd Member 2: But what about GOD'S INSTRUCTIONS?

Noah: I...I guess I thought I knew BETTER.

Crowd Member 3: Is it time to get in the BOAT yet?

Noah: Uh, not YET. ANYWAY, I started building the FIFTY-FOOT ARK, but it was going to be so EXPENSIVE! All that WOOD, and I kept wearing out my HAMMERS. So I decided to make it...a little SMALLER.

Crowd Member 2: HOW small?

Noah: Five feet.

Crowd Member 1: WHAT did you say?

Noah: FIVE FEET! I decided to make the ark FIVE FEET LONG!

Crowd Member 2: FIVE FEET? What about GOD'S INSTRUCTIONS?

Noah: I...I thought I knew BETTER.

Crowd Member 2: Better than GOD?

Noah: I GUESS so. ANYWAY, I started building the FIVE-FOOT ARK, but it was

TAKING TOO LONG. I never had TIME for FUN! So I decided to HURRY THINGS UP by making the ark...a little SMALLER.

Crowd Member 2: SMALLER? How could it GET any smaller?

Crowd Member 1: HEY, I HEARD that! Come ON, Noah! Where IS the ark, anyway? SHOW it to us!

Crowd Member 2: Yeah, SHOW it to us!

Crowd Members 1, 2, and 3: *(Speaking together)* SHOW US the ARK! SHOW US the ARK! SHOW US the ARK!

Noah: *(Waving his arms)* OK, OK! I'll SHOW you...the ARK. *(From his pocket, he takes a little toy boat and holds it up for everyone to see.)* Uh...here it IS...the ARK...right HERE.

Crowd Member 1: WHAT? How are we supposed to fit in THAT?

Crowd Member 2: And what about all these ANIMALS?

Noah: But it's a NICE little ark, don't you THINK? It's EASY to CARRY, and...

Crowd Member 1: *(Interrupting)* HEY! Is that a CLOUD I see in the sky?

Crowd Member 2: It's...it's starting to RAIN!

Crowd Member 3: So is it TIME to get in the BOAT?

Noah: *(Looking up)* YES, I'm...I'm afraid it IS. *(Pauses.)* Oh, I wish I'd FOLLOWED GOD'S INSTRUCTIONS!

Crowd Members 1, 2, and 3: *(Speaking together)* SO DO WE!

*(**Crowd Members 1, 2,** and **3** chase **Noah** off the stage.)*

To Talk About:

- How was this different from the real story of Noah? Why do you suppose the real Noah didn't act like this one?
- What kept this Noah from following God's instructions? Do the same reasons ever keep children from following God's instructions? Explain.
- Have you ever believed that God wanted you to do something, and then you didn't do it his way? What happened?
- What symbol could remind you that following God's instructions is the best thing to do? A toy boat might be one; what other ideas can you think of?

Other Topical Tie-Ins:

Noah's ark   God's wisdom   Perseverance

The Old Rabbits' Home

Topic: Easter

Scriptures You Might Read: Matthew 28:5-7; 1 Corinthians 15:17-22

The Scene: The porch of a retirement home

The Simple Setup: The characters in this skit are all rabbits; four of them parody "famous" rabbits (the Energizer batteries bunny, the Trix cereal rabbit, Bugs Bunny, and Roger Rabbit from the movie, *Who Framed Roger Rabbit*). Do what you can to make the actors look like rabbits; at the least, give them cardboard rabbit ears taped to paper headbands. Have **N.R. Jizer** wear sunglasses, and give **Stranger** a cane. Place five chairs in a row across the stage, facing the audience. Make sure your actors understand that they should use elderly voices, that "N.R. Jizer" sounds like "Energizer," and that **Plugs Bunny** talks as much like an elderly Bugs Bunny as possible. Actors of either gender could play most roles, with minor word changes. (Note: Before the performance, you may want to review the special pronunciation of some of **Plugs Bunny's** words.)

Puppet Options: This skit lends itself perfectly to puppets—if you can find five rabbit puppets. Make paper sunglasses for **N.R. Jizer** and, perhaps, paper eyeglass frames for the other rabbits. If you want to mix puppets and live actors, cast a leader as **Stranger**.

Extra Touches: If you have time, add costume and makeup details—pink noses with whiskers, buck teeth, and clothing such as suspenders and bow ties, for example—to make your actors look even more like their characters.

The Characters:

N.R. Jizer, a nonstop talker
Trixie Rabbit, who's obsessed with fruit flavors
Plugs Bunny, a hard-of-hearing wise guy
Codger Rabbit, who's cranky and feeble
Stranger, who's friendly but quiet

*(As the skit begins, all characters except **Stranger** are onstage, sitting in a row of chairs and looking into the distance.)*

N.R.:   Well, just LOOK at that SUNSET. Too bad my EYES aren't what they USED to be. Which REMINDS me of the time I was MARCHING DOWN THE HIGHWAY in the DARK, BEATING my DRUM, and a LOGGING TRUCK HIT ME. I just kept GOING and GOING and GOING...

Trixie: *(Interrupting)* Oh, don't get started on THAT again! It IS a nice sunset, though. Reminds me of a BOWL of CEREAL: RASPBERRY RED, LEMON YELLOW, ORANGE ORANGE... Ah, but THAT cereal is for KIDS! RIGHT, Plugs?

Plugs: Ehh, what's THAT, doc?

Trixie: *(Speaking louder)* I said, "ISN'T THAT RIGHT?"

Plugs: BRIGHT? YEAH, it's BRIGHT! BRIGHTEST SUNSET I've seen TODAY!

Codger: It's the ONLY sunset you've seen today! I don't know why I hang around with you GRAY HARES. I'm a MOVIE STAR! At least I was until I was FRAMED! I was FRAMED, I tell you, or my name isn't CODGER RABBIT! *(Starts coughing.)*

*(**Stranger** enters the stage, walking with a cane.)*

Stranger: HELLO! Mind if I JOIN you?

N.R.: NOPE. Are you NEW here?

Stranger: *(Sitting)* YEP, I've just RETIRED.

N.R.: Then welcome to the OLD RABBITS' HOME! I'm N.R. JIZER. *(Points at others, introducing them.)* This is TRIXIE RABBIT; that's PLUGS BUNNY; and down there is CODGER RABBIT. He used to be a MOVIE STAR, you know.

Codger: Until I was FRAMED! *(Starts coughing again.)* FRAMED, I tell you!

N.R.: And what's YOUR name, stranger?

Stranger: Oh, just call me BUNNY.

Plugs: FUNNY? What kind of name is THAT?

Stranger: BUNNY! Just call me BUNNY!

Plugs: Ehh, what's THAT, doc?

N.R.: Never MIND. Look at that SUNSET. Reminds me of the time I MARCHED around the WORLD in EIGHTEEN DAYS. Just kept BEATING that DRUM— BOOM, BOOM, BOOM! Through HURRICANES and MUDSLIDES, UNDER

WATER and over MOUNT EVEREST! Right into the SUNSET! Nothing could STOP me! I just kept GOING and GOING and GOING...

Trixie: *(Interrupting)* And you're STILL going—going ON and ON about all the UNBELIEVABLE THINGS you've done! Well, I can top THAT! I remember the time those little BRATS wouldn't let me have any of their CEREAL. Ah, that CEREAL! BLUEBERRY BLUE, GRAPE PURPLE, WATERMELON PINK...

N.R.: *(Interrupting)* Get to the POINT, WILL YOU?

Trixie: They wouldn't even let me have a TASTE! So I STUFFED THEM INTO A VAN and DROVE TO THE CEREAL FACTORY and DUMPED THEM IN THE GIANT VATS OF FOOD COLORING! THAT taught them a lesson, I'll tell YOU! They came out LIME GREEN, APRICOT GOLD, MUSHROOM GRAY...

N.R.: *(Interrupting)* ENOUGH with the COLORS! That's quite a STORY, but I'll bet PLUGS BUNNY can beat it! RIGHT, Plugs?

Plugs: Ehh, what's THAT, doc?

N.R.: *(Speaking louder)* I say, "YOU can beat THAT!"

Plugs: Eat WHAT? Not that CEREAL, I hope! It's for KIDS!

N.R.: FORGET the cereal! We want to hear a story about the MOST UNBELIEVABLE THING you've ever DONE.

Plugs: Oh! That would be the time I BOINED ELMER FLUB to a CRISP. It was the OPENING DAY of WABBIT...I mean RABBIT HUNTING SEASON. I was MUNCHING CARROTS, MINDING my own BUSINESS, when suddenly my whole WOILD exploded! Old ELMER was SHOOTING at me! So I TOINED, and with all my STRENGTH, I reached up and TIED HIS SHOTGUN IN A KNOT. Next time he FIRED, he was TOAST.

Codger: *(Speaking loudly)* What's so unbelievable about THAT? MY story is the UNBELIEVABLE one.

Plugs: Oh, YEAH? What's YOUR story, doc?

Codger: *(Pauses.)* I was FRAMED!

**N.R., Trixie,
and Plugs:** *(Speaking together)* We KNOW!

N.R.: *(Speaking to **Stranger**)* How about YOU, newcomer? What's the most unbelievable thing YOU'VE ever done?

Stranger: *(Pauses.)* HMM, I guess that would BE...EASTER.

Trixie: EASTER? What ABOUT it?

Stranger: Well, I managed to CONVINCE everybody that it was REALLY about...COLORED EGGS.

N.R.: WHAT?

Trixie: COLORED EGGS?

Codger: You're KIDDING!

Plugs: That's the most RIDICULOUS thing I ever HOID!

N.R.: Now LISTEN, stranger. We like to tell some TALL TALES around here. But that whopper YOU just told is a little TOO unbelievable!

Codger: YEAH! Who would fall for a story that said EASTER was about COLORED EGGS?

Stranger: Oh, you'd be SURPRISED.

Plugs: And I suppose you got everybody to FORGET about the REAL meaning of Easter?

N.R.: About that MAN who DIED, then came BACK and just kept GOING and GOING and GOING?

Stranger: That's RIGHT.

Codger: *(Getting up)* Well, you can't expect us to believe THAT, pal. We weren't born YESTERDAY, you know!

N.R.: *(Getting up)* Not by a LONG shot!

Plugs: *(Getting up)* Colored EGGS, my FOOT! What's up with THAT, doc?

N.R.: Well, it's time to get inside for DINNER. Probably MASHED CARROTS again.

*(All groan and exit the stage except for **Trixie** and **Stranger**, who talk on their way out.)*

Trixie: SAY, bunny, these COLORED EGGS—were they RASPBERRY RED?

Stranger: YUP.

Trixie: LEMON YELLOW?

Stranger: YEP.

Trixie: ORANGE ORANGE?

Stranger: You GOT it.

Trixie: OOH… *(Exits the stage.)*

Stranger: Gets 'em every TIME! *(Exits the stage.)*

To Talk About:

- About how old were you when you first heard of the Easter bunny? What did you think when you heard about him?
- Which do you suppose more people think of when they hear the word "Easter": colored eggs or Jesus? Why?
- What do you think is the best way to celebrate Easter? Why?
- In no more than ten words, how would you explain to someone who'd never heard of Easter why it's important?

Other Topical Tie-Ins:

Faith   Jesus' resurrection   Who to listen to

Out-of-State Plates

Topic: What Heaven Is Like

Scriptures You Might Read: Revelation 7:9-17; 22:1-6

The Scene: The back seat of a moving car

The Simple Setup: Place two chairs at center stage to represent a car seat. Both actors may wear casual clothes.

Puppet Options: You could use puppets for both roles. If you want to mix puppets and live actors, cast a child in the role of **Sister**.

Extra Touches: A simple backdrop showing a car's rear window from the inside would help to identify the setting.

The Characters:
Sister, a girl who doesn't think for herself
Brother, a boy with the same problem

*(As the skit begins, **Sister** and **Brother** are seated next to each other.)*

Brother:		Sis, this VACATION TRIP is so LONG and BORING! We should have gone to the GRAND CANYON instead!
Sister:		How COME?
Brother:		Because they have GIANT FROGS that GLOW IN THE DARK and WHISTLE THE SONG from *Rugrats*!
Sister:		REALLY?
Brother:		HEY, I saw it on TV!
Sister:		Oh. WELL, then, it MUST be true.
Brother:		Let's play a GAME.

Sister: What do you want to PLAY?

Brother: TOUCH FOOTBALL.

Sister: TOUCH FOOTBALL? We're riding in the BACK SEAT of the CAR!

Brother: OK, OK, let's play the LICENSE PLATE GAME.

*(**Brother** and **Sister** pretend to look out the car windows.)*

Brother: I see a license plate from…NEW JERSEY!

Sister: I see a license plate from…OKLAHOMA!

Brother: I see a license plate from…HEAVEN!

Sister: WHAT?

Brother: I see a license plate from HEAVEN!

Sister: WHERE?

Brother: On that YELLOW CAR down the ROAD!

Sister: It's already TOO FAR AWAY! I can't SEE!

Brother: The license plate said "HEAVEN"! REALLY! *(Turning toward the "front seat")* DAD, you've got to CATCH UP with that YELLOW CAR!

Sister: WOW! What do you suppose a car from HEAVEN is doing HERE?

Brother: DUH! OBVIOUSLY it's an ANGEL DRIVING ACROSS THE COUNTRY to HELP LITTLE KIDS WIN THEIR SOCCER GAMES.

Sister: How do you KNOW?

Brother: HEY, I saw it on TV.

Sister: Oh. WELL, then it MUST be true.

Brother: Of course, I saw this OTHER TV show where an angel had WINGS and could FLY anywhere he wanted.

Sister: So, does THAT mean...

Brother: (Interrupting) On the OTHER hand, I saw this OTHER TV show where this guy got SENT FROM HEAVEN to do GOOD DEEDS, and HE drove a MOTORCYCLE. So why not a CAR?

Sister: Uh...YEAH. THAT makes sense. (Pauses.) I wonder what heaven is LIKE?

Brother: Hey, EVERYBODY knows THAT! Heaven is full of PEOPLE IN WHITE ROBES sitting around on CLOUDS. They play HARPS, and they have HALOS over their HEADS.

Sister: Did you see that on...

Brother: TV!

Sister: WELL, then it MUST be true. (Pauses.) But is THAT all we get to DO in heaven? Sit around on CLOUDS and play HARPS?

Brother: Are you KIDDING? In HEAVEN you get to do ANYTHING you WANT—eat all the JUNK FOOD you want, play all the VIDEO GAMES you want. It's like DISNEY WORLD but with NO LINES.

Sister: Are you SURE?

Brother: HEY, I saw it...

Sister: ...on TV?

Brother: No, in a MOVIE!

Sister: Oh. WELL, then it REALLY must be true! (Pauses, looking out her "window.") I wish there was a way to find out MORE about heaven. Like, if somebody had actually SEEN it and WROTE about it in a BOOK.

Brother: A BOOK? About HEAVEN?

Sister: Yeah.

Brother: A book that tells about GOD, and what he's LIKE, and how to BE with him FOREVER?

Sister: YEAH.

Brother: There's NO SUCH BOOK.

Sister: How do you KNOW?

Brother: I NEVER saw it on TV.

Sister: Oh.

Brother: OR in a MOVIE!

Sister: WELL, then the book MUST not exist.

Brother: BESIDES we've ALREADY got a way to find out all about HEAVEN. We can ask that guy in the YELLOW CAR! *(Speaking to the "front seat")* Come ON, Dad! FASTER! We've got to CATCH UP!

Sister: We're almost THERE! *(Leans forward to look out the "window.")* I can just about read the... HEY! THAT license plate doesn't say "HEAVEN."

Brother: HUH?

Sister: It says..."HAWAII"!

Brother: HAWAII? *(Looks out the "window")* Uh...I guess you're RIGHT.

Sister: *(Resting back in her seat)* Now I'll NEVER know what heaven is like.

Brother: Not unless you find that BOOK about it!

Sister: And THAT'S not going to happen.

Brother: So let's talk about HAWAII instead. I hear they have PINEAPPLES as big as VOLCANOES!

*(**Brother** and **Sister** pretend to get out of the car. They begin walking off the stage.)*

Sister: WHAT?

Brother: HEY, I saw it in a COMIC BOOK!

Sister: Oh. WELL, then it MUST be true!

(**Brother** and **Sister** exit the stage.)

● **To Talk About:**

- Have you wondered what heaven is like? If so, what caused you to start thinking about it?
- How do people spend their time in heaven? How do you know?
- Are TV shows and movies good places to learn about heaven? Why or why not?
- Do you feel "ready" to live in heaven? Does the idea of living that close to God make you nervous, happy, bored, or something else?

● **Other Topical Tie-Ins:**

The Bible's authority   Entertainment   The supernatural

Squeal of Fortune

Topic: Watching Your Words

Scriptures You Might Read: Proverbs 15:1-2; James 3:3-12

The Scene: A TV studio

The Simple Setup: You'll need chalkboard and chalk or a flip chart and a marker. Set these at center stage. **Brat** should stand toward stage left, near the two contestants. **Announcer** should stand at stage right—behind a microphone stand, if you like. You'll also need an offstage sound effects helper with a buzzer and a bell. A board game buzzer would work well, or the sound effects helper could make the noise vocally. The bell should be a desk-style bell or a tricycle bell. Give **Announcer** a sign that says "Squeal of Fortune" on one side and "Applause" on the other. Explain to audience members that they'll be shouting "Squeal of Fortune" or applauding as cued by the sign. All actors could get by with casual clothes. If possible, have **Banana** wear a flashy outfit and have **Brat** wear a suit. **Banana** will need something with which to cover **Brat's** mouth at the end of the skit; try a scarf or a piece of not-too-sticky tape.

Puppet Options: You could use puppets for all the roles. If **Banana** is a puppet, write the puzzle on the board before the skit. If you want to mix puppets and live actors, cast a leader as **Announcer**.

Extra Touches: For that total game show feeling, play a little upbeat music at the beginning and end of the skit.

The Characters:
Brat Stayback, a temperamental game show host
Barbie Malibu, a silly contestant
Alfred Einstein, an overly serious contestant
Banana Brite, a glamorous assistant
Announcer

*(As the skit begins, only **Announcer** is onstage.)*

Announcer: From PHONY STUDIOS, it's the GAME SHOW that's SWEEPING THE NATION...UNDER THE RUG! It's... *(Holds up "Squeal of Fortune" sign.)*

Audience: ..."SQUEAL OF FORTUNE"!

Announcer: And here's your HOST, a man who knows how to watch EVERYBODY'S words, BRAT STAYBACK! (*Holds up "Applause" sign and motions for audience to applaud.*)

Brat: (*Entering the stage*) HI, everybody, and welcome to "SQUEAL OF FORTUNE"! Let's say hello to our lovely LETTER-WRITER, Ms. BANANA BRITE!

(**Banana** enters the stage and waves.)

(**Announcer** holds up "Applause" sign.)

Brat: And now let's meet our CONTESTANTS!

Announcer: Brat, our FIRST player comes from MALIBU BARBIE, CALIFORNIA! Her HOBBIES are LOOKING IN THE MIRROR and...LOOKING IN THE MIRROR SOME MORE! Let's welcome BARBIE MALIBU! (*Holds up "Applause" sign.*)

(**Barbie** enters the stage and waves.)

Brat: HI, Barbie! What's on your MIND?

Barbie: NOTHING!

Brat: That's what I THOUGHT. And who's our OTHER contestant?

Announcer: Brat, our SECOND player comes from a DUSTY OLD SHELF in the BASEMENT of a SCIENCE LAB somewhere in northern IDAHO. His HOBBIES are COMPUTERS and...MORE computers! Say hello to ALFRED EINSTEIN! (*Holds up "Applause" sign.*)

(**Alfred** enters the stage and waves.)

Brat: HI, Al! What's UP?

Alfred: Layers of AIR.

Brat: Uh...RIGHT. OK, players! YOU know how to play "SQUEAL OF FORTUNE." You keep buying LETTERS to complete a PHRASE, and when you're ready to GUESS the phrase—SQUEAL! Let's hear you SQUEAL!

Barbie: (*Squealing*) EEEEE!

Brat: GOOD! Al?

Alfred: (*Grunting*) UNNH.

Brat: Sounds more like a GRUNT, but it'll do. BANANA, please go to the BOARD and START our PUZZLE.

(**Banana** *walks to chalkboard and writes* "W_TCH Y_ _ R W_RDS.")

Brat: And there's the PHRASE. No help from the AUDIENCE, please! Barbie, let's begin with YOU.

Barbie: Um, I'd like to buy a C, Brat!

(*Offstage helper sounds the buzzer.*)

Brat: SORRY, Barbie! No C. Al?

Alfred: I wish to purchase a C, Brat.

(*Offstage helper sounds the buzzer.*)

Brat: But she just BOUGHT a C, Alfred!

Alfred: She DID?

Brat: YES! Now pay ATTENTION, BALLOON BRAIN!

(*Offstage helper sounds the buzzer.*)

Brat: Oh. The JUDGES are warning me to WATCH MY WORDS. OK. YOUR turn, Barbie.

Barbie: Um, I'd like to buy a D, Brat.

(*Offstage helper sounds the buzzer.*)

Brat: A D? What kind of choice was THAT?

(*Offstage helper sounds the buzzer.*)

Brat: There's no WAY a D could fit in there!

(*Offstage helper sounds the buzzer twice.*)

Brat: Oh, never MIND. YOUR turn, Alfred.

Alfred: Is there...an X?

(Offstage helper sounds the buzzer.)

Brat: X? An X? Why don't you buy a VOWEL? A VOWEL! A-E-I-O-U and sometimes Y! I thought this guy was supposed to be a GENIUS!

(Offstage helper sounds the buzzer.)

Brat: Oh, be QUIET!

(Offstage helper sounds the buzzer three times.)

Brat: Barbie, I'd say it was your TURN, but you'd probably ask me where the STEERING WHEEL was!

(Offstage helper sounds the buzzer four times.)

Barbie: Brat, I'd like to SOLVE the PUZZLE.

Brat: FINALLY! What's the ANSWER?

Barbie: I don't KNOW. I'd LIKE to solve the puzzle, but I don't know the ANSWER.

Brat: AARGH! I can't BELIEVE this! Where did we GET these contestants?

Announcer: Brat, our FIRST player comes from MALIBU BARBIE, CALIFORNIA! And our SECOND player comes from a DUSTY OLD SHELF in the BASEMENT of...

Brat: *(Interrupting)* SHUT UP! Just SHUT UP!

(Offstage helper sounds the buzzer.)

Brat: These players are NEVER going to solve the puzzle! They probably couldn't guess their own NAMES!

(Offstage helper sounds the buzzer twice.)

Alfred: Uh, is my name BENJAMIN FRANKLIN?

(Offstage helper sounds the buzzer.)

Brat: SEE? These people are such CLOWNS!

(Offstage helper sounds the buzzer.)

Brat: Everyone I WORK with is a clown!

(Offstage helper sounds the buzzer twice.)

Brat: The JUDGES are clowns!

(Offstage helper sounds the buzzer three times.)

Brat: The AUDIENCE is a BUNCH of clowns!

*(Offstage helper sounds the buzzer four times. **Banana** angrily leaves the chalkboard and walks over to **Brat**.)*

Banana: OK, Brat! That's the LAST STRAW! You're always watching OTHER people's words, but you don't watch your OWN!

(Offstage helper rings the bell three times.)

Banana: SEE? The JUDGES AGREE!

(Offstage helper rings the bell eight times.)

Banana: No more words from YOU, Brat!

*(**Banana** takes out the gag or tape and starts to put it over **Brat's** mouth.)*

Brat: WHAT? HEY! You can't DO this!

*(Offstage helper rings the bell ten times as **Banana** successfully puts the gag or tape over **Brat's** mouth. **Announcer** holds up "Applause" sign as **Brat** stamps his feet. **Barbie** and **Alfred** join in the applause.)*

Brat: MMPH! MMPH!

Banana: WELL folks, we've run out of TIME. So let's just have our AUDIENCE solve the puzzle! What do you think the phrase IS, everyone? *(Pauses for audience to respond.)* That's RIGHT! "WATCH YOUR WORDS"! So until NEXT time, WATCH YOUR WORDS. And don't forget to watch...

*(**Announcer** holds up "Squeal of Fortune" sign.)*

Audience: "SQUEAL OF FORTUNE"!

(**Announcer** *holds up "Applause" sign. Offstage helper rings the bell at least twelve times as* **Banana, Barbie, Alfred,** *and* **Announcer** *lead the protesting* **Brat** *offstage.*)

● To Talk About:

· What does it mean to watch your words? Why bother to do it?

· If you had a dollar for every mean thing people have said to you, how much do you think you'd have? If you had to pay a dollar for every mean thing you've ever said, how much do you think you'd owe?

· Is calling people names like "clown" and "balloon brain" ever really funny? Why or why not? If something seems funny to you, is it OK to say it? Why or why not?

· In our group, how can we help each other know when words are hurtful?

● Other Topical Tie-Ins:

Taming the tongue   Hurtful humor   Respecting one another

Star Chores

Topic: Listening to Wisdom

Scriptures You Might Read: Proverbs 2:1-6; 3:1-6

The Scene: A planet in a galaxy far, far away

The Simple Setup: This is a parody of the *Star Wars* movies. No set is required. **Luke** needs a prop resembling a hand-held video game (a calculator will do). You'll also want "light sabers" for **Luke** and **Darth** (use the plastic "sabers" available in toy stores, or just use long cardboard tubes). **Princess Fleeya** stays offstage, out of sight. (Note: Make sure **Luke** knows that **Obi** is pronounced "O-bee.")

Puppet Options: For **Luke**, you can use any boy puppet. An adult male Bible-times puppet with a robe, beard, and so on would make a good **Obi**. Any adult male puppet can serve as **Darth**. If you want a live actor to interact with the puppets, cast a leader as **Obi**. Use downsized props—a small piece of cardboard for the video game and pencils for light sabers, for example—with the puppets.

Extra Touches: If you like, costume your actors. Have **Luke** wear a karate uniform or white bathrobe. Provide a robe and hood for **Obi** and a dark robe for **Darth**. To create even more atmosphere, open and close the skit with a few bars of the *Star Wars* theme song.

The Characters:

    Luke Skygazer, a young video game player
    Obi Macaroni, his wise old teacher
    Princess Fleeya, the ruler of the planet
    Darth Shaver, an evil warrior

(As the skit begins, **Luke** *enters, pretending to play a hand-held video game.)*

Obi: *(Entering the stage)* Ah, young LUKE SKYGAZER!

Luke: *(Still playing the video game)* HUH? WHAT?

Obi: I'm GLAD you have COME, Luke. I need your HELP.

Luke: *(Looking up)* Oh, it's YOU, OBI MACARONI. *(Goes back to playing, continues to play until further notice.)* I'm kind of BUSY with this GAME GUY. I just got to the THREE HUNDREDTH LEVEL of DINKY KONG ONE THOUSAND.

Obi: Luke, this is much more IMPORTANT than a VIDEO GAME. I have received a MESSAGE from PRINCESS FLEEYA.

Luke: WHO?

Obi: Princess FLEEYA. YOU know, the RULER of our PLANET who wears a WHITE ROBE and HAIR rolled up like DOUGHNUTS on the sides of her HEAD.

Luke: HUH? A PLANET with HAIR rolled up like DOUGHNUTS?

Obi: Luke, you must pay ATTENTION. We are all in great DANGER.

Luke: Uh, DANGER. Yeah.

Obi: Do you want to hear the MESSAGE?

Luke: WHAT message?

Obi: The one from Princess FLEEYA! She left it on my ANSWERING MACHINE.

(**Obi** *pretends to take a device from his pocket and push a button on it. When he does,* **Princess Fleeya** *calls from offstage.*)

Fleeya: (*Speaking from offstage*) HELP me, Obi Macaroni! The evil warrior DARTH SHAVER plans to DESTROY our PLANET! HELP me, Obi Macaroni! You're my only HOPE! HELP me, Obi Macaroni! You're my only HOPE!

Luke: Does she always REPEAT herself like that?

Obi: Luke, this is SERIOUS. I must prepare you to BATTLE DARTH SHAVER. I must TEACH you to become a RED-EYE KNIGHT.

Luke: A WHAT?

Obi: A RED-EYE KNIGHT! Here, take this LIGHT SABER.

(**Obi** *offers* **Luke** *the "saber."* **Luke** *finally puts down his video game and takes the saber.*)

Luke: WHOA! COOL! How does this thing WORK? Where's the START button?

Obi: It HAS no buttons, Luke. To make it work, you must USE THE SOURCE.

Luke: The WHAT?

Obi: The SOURCE! The greatest power in the UNIVERSE—GOD'S power!

Luke: YEAH, yeah, OK. Whatever. *(Puts down the saber and picks up the video game.)* I've got to finish this GAME first, though. *(Plays the game until further notice.)*

Obi: Luke, you're not LISTENING! You must learn to USE THE SOURCE!

Luke: Right. DON'T worry, I'll REMEMBER. MAN, this game is HARD! I only have THREE LIVES left!

Obi: You're going to NEED them.

Luke: HUH?

Obi: He's HERE, Luke.

Luke: WHO'S here?

Obi: DARTH SHAVER. I can FEEL it.

Luke: Uh, why don't YOU fight him? I've got to finish this GAME.

Obi: NO, Luke. I am an OLD MAN. The SOURCE is STRONG in you—if you know how to USE it.

Luke: Hmm? Use WHAT?

Obi: He's COMING, Luke. REMEMBER, use the SOURCE! *(Exits the stage.)*

Luke: Uh, WHAT did you say?

Darth: *(Entering the stage, holding a saber of his own)* SO, young Skygazer! Have you become a RED-EYE KNIGHT?

Luke: *(Putting down the video game and picking up the saber)* Uh, YEAH. Sort of.

Darth: Then PREPARE to MEET your DOOM!

Luke: Um, I think you forgot your HELMET.

Darth: WHAT? You dare INSULT the great DARTH SHAVER? You will be SORRY, young Red-Eye Knight! *(Threatens **Luke** with the saber.)*

Luke: *(Speaking to himself)* Oh MAN, what did Obi Macaroni say to DO? Use the...use the...

Obi: *(Speaking from offstage)* Use the SOURCE, Luke!

Luke: That's IT! USE the HORSE!

Darth: The HORSE?

Luke: WAIT a minute. I don't HAVE a horse.

Obi: *(Speaking from offstage)* The SOURCE, Luke! Use the SOURCE!

Luke: The FORK? Use the FORK?

Darth: The FORK? WHAT am I, a SALAD?

Luke: Oh, MAN HELP me, Obi Macaroni! HELP me, Obi Macaroni! *(Runs off the stage, going to the side opposite the side **Obi** used to exit.)*

Darth: Does he ALWAYS repeat himself like that? *(Runs after **Luke**.)*

*(**Obi** enters the stage, shaking his head.)*

Obi: Ah well, nobody LISTENS to me anymore. *(Picks up the video game.)* Looks like...GAME'S OVER! *(Exits the stage.)*

● **To Talk About:**
- Why didn't Luke listen to Obi? What kinds of things keep the kids you know from listening to good advice?
- What do you think it means to be wise? Who's the wisest person you know? Why?
- What's the best piece of advice you've ever heard from the Bible? Do you think most kids follow that advice? Why or why not?
- What do you think might happen if you remembered to "use the Source"—God's power—the next time you face a problem at school? How could you go about it?

● **Other Topical Tie-Ins:**

God's power   Spiritual warfare   Entertainment   Respecting elders

The Sword Drill

Topic: Practicing What You Preach

Scriptures You Might Read: James 1:22-25; 1 John 3:18

The Scene: An auditorium platform

The Simple Setup: You'll need two chairs and three large Bibles. Actors of either gender could play all roles, with minor word changes. All actors should wear "Sunday best" clothes.

Puppet Options: You could use puppets for all the roles. If you use puppets, use small Bibles and make sure the puppets' hands can turn a few pages. The part of **Emcee** would be a natural for an adult leader if you desire interaction between puppets and live actors.

Extra Touches: If possible, display a trophy onstage as if it were to be awarded to the winner of the sword drill.

The Characters:
> Kid 1, who's bent on winning at any cost
> Kid 2, who's much like **Kid 1**
> Emcee, a reasonable adult

*(As the skit begins, **Kids 1** and **2** are sitting in chairs near the center of the stage, facing the audience. **Emcee** is standing between them. Each character holds a large Bible.)*

Emcee: LADIES and GENTLEMEN, WELCOME to the TENTH ANNUAL SUPER SWORD DRILL! As you KNOW, our CONTESTANTS have been practicing EVERY DAY for the last YEAR, and now they can find ANY BIBLE VERSE in a matter of SECONDS! TELL me, contestants, what's the SECRET to finding Bible verses so QUICKLY?

Kid 1:   It's all in the WRIST.

Kid 2:   No, it's all in the FINGERS.

Kid 1:   WRIST!

Kid 2:   FINGERS!

Emcee: Uh, OK, let's get STARTED. You all know the RULES. When I call out a verse and say, "READY, SET, GO," you FIND it. The first one to STAND UP and READ THE VERSE WINS that ROUND! The person to win the MOST rounds gets the CHAMPIONSHIP TROPHY! Any QUESTIONS?

Kid 2: YEAH. *(Pointing at Kid 1)* Who's going to watch and make sure he doesn't CHEAT?

Kid 1: ME? Who's going to watch YOU?

Emcee: Er, our JUDGES will be watching. But I'm sure NO ONE'S going to cheat, right? I mean, this IS a contest using the BIBLE!

Kid 1: Tell HIM that!

Kid 2: *(Speaking to Kid 1)* Tell YOURSELF!

Emcee: Uh, GREAT! Let's BEGIN! Here's the VERSE: Romans 12:10! Ready, set, GO!

(Kids 1 and 2 flip through their Bibles. In a few seconds. Kid 1 stands.)

Kid 1: "Be DEVOTED to one another in BROTHERLY LOVE. HONOR one another above YOURSELVES" (Romans 12:10)! *(Sits.)*

Kid 2: He CHEATED!

Kid 1: I did NOT!

Emcee: Um, that is the CORRECT VERSE. And an IMPORTANT one it IS, too, about LOVING each other and...

Kid 2: *(Interrupting)* Come ON, let's have the NEXT verse! I'm already BEHIND!

Kid 1: And you're gonna STAY that way!

Kid 2: Why, I oughta...

Emcee: *(Interrupting)* NEXT verse! Proverbs 14:29! Ready, set, GO!

(Kids 1 and 2 flip through their Bibles. In a few seconds. Kid 2 stands.)

Kid 2: "A PATIENT man has great UNDERSTANDING, but a QUICK-TEMPERED man displays FOLLY" (Proverbs 14:29)! *(Sits.)*

Kid 1: CHEATER! You LICKED your FINGERS!

Kid 2: I did NOT!

Emcee: Uh, that verse is CORRECT. So let's ALL remember to be PATIENT instead of QUICK-TEMPERED.

Kid 1: (Speaking to **Kid 2**) FINGER LICKER!

Kid 2: (Speaking to **Kid 1**) NOSE PICKER!

Emcee: Uh, on to the NEXT verse, James 3:9-10! Ready, set, GO!

(**Kids 1** and **2** flip through their Bibles. In a few seconds, **Kid 1** stands.)

Kid 1: "With the TONGUE we PRAISE our Lord and FATHER, and with it we CURSE MEN, who have been made in God's LIKENESS. Out of the SAME MOUTH come PRAISE and CURSING. My BROTHERS, this should not BE" (James 3:9-10)! (Sits.)

Emcee: That is CORRECT!

Kid 2: What a GREAT VERSE! Too bad it had to be read by YOU!

Emcee: Now that's EXACTLY what the verse is TALKING about...

Kid 1: (Interrupting, speaking to **Kid 2**) Well, you shouldn't even be allowed to TOUCH this HOLY BOOK!

Emcee: Uh, the score is TWO to ONE! Let's continue with Romans 12:17. Ready, set, GO!

(**Kids 1** and **2** flip through their Bibles. In a few seconds, **Kid 2** stands.)

Kid 2: "Do not REPAY anyone EVIL for EVIL. Be careful to do what is right in the eyes of everybody" (Romans 12:17)! (Sits.)

Kid 1: I'm gonna GET you for that!

Kid 2: Not if I get you FIRST!

Emcee: The verse is CORRECT. But I MUST ask the contestants to...

Kid 1: (Interrupting, speaking to **Kid 2**) Why don't you step OUTSIDE?

Kid 2: (Speaking to **Kid 1**) Why don't you MAKE me?

Emcee: I MUST ask the contestants NOT to repay anyone EVIL for EVIL. *(Pauses.)* Now let's move to the NEXT verse, 1 John 3:18. Ready, set, GO!

*(**Kids 1** and **2** flip through their Bibles. In a few seconds, **Kid 2** stands.)*

Kid 2: "For GOD so loved the WORLD that he gave his one and only SON, that whoever BELIEVES in him shall not PERISH but have ETERNAL LIFE" (John 3:16)! *(Sits.)*

Emcee: I'm SORRY. That is NOT the correct verse.

Kid 2: WHAT?

Kid 1: *(Standing)* He said John 3:18—"Whoever BELIEVES in him is not CONDEMNED, but whoever does NOT believe..."

Emcee: *(Interrupting)* I'm SORRY. THAT is not the correct verse, EITHER.

Kid 1: WHAT?

Emcee: *(Looking in the Bible)* The CORRECT verse is 1 John 3:18—"Dear CHILDREN, let us not love with WORDS or TONGUE but with ACTIONS and in TRUTH."

Kids 1 and 2: *(Speaking together)* ACTIONS and TRUTH?

Kid 2: What do THEY have to do with anything?

Kid 1: What a DUMB VERSE! No WONDER I couldn't find it!

Kid 2: This is the WORST sword drill I ever SAW! I'm QUITTING!

Kid 1: Me, TOO!

Emcee: But WAIT! You can't...

Kid 1: I'm going to enter the BIBLE MEMORY CONTEST instead! I've got 1 Corinthians 13:4 MEMORIZED!

Kid 2: Who DOESN'T? "Love is PATIENT, love is KIND. It does not BOAST, it does not ENVY..."

Kid 1: NO, it's "Love is PATIENT, love never FAILS. It does not ENVY, it is not PROUD..."

Kid 2: *(Starting to exit the stage)* LOVE is KIND!

Kid 1: *(Starting to exit the stage)* LOVE never FAILS!

*(**Kids 1** and **2** exit the stage.)*

Emcee: *(Sighs.)* Well, I only had ONE MORE VERSE. *(Looking in the Bible)* James 1:22—"Do not merely LISTEN to the word, and so DECEIVE yourselves. Do what it SAYS." *(Sighs again.)* I guess when we forget THAT verse, EVERYBODY loses. *(Exits the stage.)*

● **To Talk About:**

- Do you think it's more important to *know* a Bible verse or to *obey* it? Can you really do one without the other? Explain.
- What does it mean to "practice what you preach"? If you're not a good "practicer," should you just quit "preaching"? Why or why not?
- What would be your advice to the contestants in the skit?
- Do you need to learn more Bible verses, obey the ones you already know, or both? Why?

● **Other Topical Tie-Ins:**

Loving one another   Memorizing the Bible   Obeying God

A Tall Tale

Topic: Self-Esteem

Scriptures You Might Read: Matthew 6:25-26; Luke 19:1-10

The Scene: A Jericho road

The Simple Setup: Put a sturdy table to one side of the stage to serve as the "tree" **Zaccheus** climbs. Have **Zaccheus** and **Marcus** wear robes and headgear (towels held with bandannas). Have **Offstage Heckler** and **Voice of Jesus** use microphones and deliver their lines from offstage, if possible. When casting the two main characters, keep in mind that, while **Zaccheus** need not be unusually short, **Marcus** should be noticeably taller. (Note: Before the performance, you may want to make sure actors are familiar with the word "periscope.")

Puppet Options: Use Bible-character puppets for **Zaccheus** and **Marcus** if you'd like. Or cast a leader as **Marcus** to interact with the puppet **Zaccheus**. If **Zaccheus** is a puppet, you may want to make a cardboard tree for him to climb.

Extra Touches: If you'd like to involve more kids, cast several as crowd members to mill around in front of the "tree."

The Characters:
> **Zaccheus**, a "vertically challenged" tax collector and basketball fan
> **Marcus**, his wise friend
> **Offstage Heckler**, who's mean and taunting
> **Voice of Jesus**, who's warm and kind

*(As the skit begins, **Zaccheus** is pretending to dribble and shoot a basketball.)*

Zack: He SHOOTS…he SCORES! And the crowd goes WILD for number X…X…I…I…I!

Marcus: *(Entering the stage)* HI, Zaccheus! Still dreaming of being a BASKETBALL PLAYER, eh?

Zack: DREAMING? I'm GOING to be a basketball player, Marcus! I'm going to be the GREATEST CENTER in the history of the NBA!

Marcus: NBA? What's THAT?

Zack: The NAZARETH BASKETBALL ASSOCIATION.

Marcus: Zack, I hate to BREAK this to you. But every basketball star I'VE ever seen is TALL. REALLY tall. About FIVE CUBITS tall.

Zack: SO?

Marcus: Well, you're really…uh…NOT tall.

Zack: Go ahead, SAY it! You think I'm SHORT, DON'T you?

Marcus: Well…

Offstage Heckler: Hey, SHRIMP! Why don't you CLIMB a LADDER and CLIP my TOENAILS?

Marcus: Maybe he meant ME.

Zack: No PROBLEM! People can make fun of me all they WANT. Pretty soon they won't get to DO it anymore.

Marcus: Why NOT?

Zack: Because… *(pretends to shoot a basketball)* I'm about to get TALL!

Marcus: Get TALL? HOW?

Zack: You've heard of that MIRACLE WORKER, JESUS, right? Well, he's coming here to JERICHO today. And he's going to make me TALL.

Marcus: Make you TALL? Why would he do THAT?

Zack: Because he FIXES people! He's made the LAME WALK, helped the BLIND SEE, even RAISED the DEAD. Making me TALL enough for the NBA should be EASY.

Marcus: But ZACK, think of the CROWDS! You're so…UNTALL that you won't even be able to SEE when Jesus is walking BY.

Zack: HEY, I've got it COVERED. I'll use…STILTS!

Marcus: No, too DANGEROUS.

Zack: How about ELEVATOR SANDALS?

Marcus: Not HIGH enough.

Zack: I've GOT it! I'll see over people's HEADS with a PERISCOPE.

Marcus: SORRY. Periscopes haven't been INVENTED yet.

Zack: Oh. Then how am I going to see JESUS? I've got to get his ATTENTION so he'll make me SUPER TALL.

Marcus: Well, there IS that SYCAMORE TREE over there. *(Points at table.)*

Zack: That's IT! I'll climb the SYCAMORE TREE.

Marcus: But, ZACK...

Zack: *(Interrupting)* Come ON! Let's BEAT the CROWD!

*(**Zack** runs over to the table and climbs on it. **Marcus** stands next to table.)*

Zack: WOW! What a VIEW!

Offstage Heckler: Hey, SHORTY! Why is a NUT like YOU growing on a SYCAMORE tree?

Zack: LAUGH it UP! In a couple of minutes, you'll wish YOU could be as high as my KNEECAPS!

Marcus: Zack, I'm SORRY some people give you a HARD TIME because of your SIZE.

Zack: Yeah, me TOO. But soon that'll be OVER. When Jesus makes me tall enough to be a BASKETBALL PLAYER, everyone will LOOK UP to me.

Marcus: WELL I...

Zack: *(Interrupting)* At LAST people will RESPECT me! Because I'll be WORTH something!

Marcus: Zack, you're ALREADY worth something! GOD made you the way you ARE, and what HE makes is NEVER WORTHLESS.

Zack: YEAH, yeah. YOU'LL see. When Jesus notices how SHORT I am, HE'LL know a MISTAKE'S been made! He'll FIX me, and then I'll be... *(Looks into distance.)* Hey, LOOK! Here comes JESUS! *(Pause.)* HI, Jesus! Up HERE! In the TREE! It's ME, ZACCHEUS! I'm your BIGGEST FAN! Well, maybe your SMALLEST fan...

Voice of Jesus: ZACCHEUS, come down IMMEDIATELY! I must stay at your HOUSE today.

Zack: HUH? Marcus, how can he come to my HOUSE? Can't he see that I don't DESERVE such an HONOR? It's not like I'm a BASKETBALL PLAYER or anything. I'm just a guy who's too SHORT!

Marcus: Maybe that's not ALL you are, Zack. Maybe Jesus knows what you're really WORTH.

Zack: WOW! *(Calling to the unseen Jesus)* OK, Jesus, I'll be GLAD to have you over at my house! Maybe we can play a little ONE-ON-ONE! *(Getting down from the table)* Let's GO, Marcus! I've got to SET THE TABLE!

Marcus: *(Speaking as they start to leave)* WELL, Zack, I hope you're not too DISAPPOINTED that Jesus didn't CHANGE YOUR HEIGHT.

Zack: Marcus, what are you TALKING about? Of COURSE he changed my height.

Marcus: He DID?

Zack: SURE! Thanks to JESUS, I feel TEN FEET TALL!

*(**Zack** and **Marcus** exit the stage.)*

To Talk About:

- Would you rather change your name, give yourself one ability you don't have now, or change one thing about your looks? Why?
- Read the story of the real Zaccheus in Luke 19:1-10. How is the skit like the true story? How is it different?
- Why do you suppose Jesus went to Zaccheus' home? What did Jesus know about Zaccheus that nobody else did?
- What could Jesus say to you that would make you feel "ten feet tall"? How has he already said something like that in Matthew 6:25-26, John 15:14 and other Bible passages?

Other Topical Tie-Ins:

Accepting others   Miracles   Getting to know Jesus

Trivial Pursuit

Topic: Learning God's Word

Scriptures You Might Read: Psalm 119:9-11, 36-37

The Scene: A living room

The Simple Setup: No set or props are required. Both characters should wear casual clothes. The door through which **Tracy** enters can be real or imaginary. If **Tracy** doesn't make the knocking sound, an offstage helper could do so. Actors of either gender could play both roles, with minor word changes.

Puppet Options: You could use puppets for both roles. If you want to mix puppets and live actors, cast a leader or child in the role of **Tracy**.

Extra Touches: If you'd like, you could put a real TV on the floor with the picture facing away from the audience.

The Characters:
      Eddie, a kid obsessed with a TV super-hero team
      Tracy, Eddie's levelheaded friend

*(As the skit begins, **Eddie** is sitting on the floor, watching an imaginary TV and talking back to it.)*

Eddie: YEAH! GO, you TURBO MORPHIN' DANGER LIZARDS! Go, PURPLE Lizard! Go, ORANGE Lizard! Go, SLIGHTLY GREENISH-YELLOW Lizard!

(Offstage helper knocks.)

Eddie: Go, OFF-WHITE Lizard! Go, GLOW-IN-THE-DARK Lizard!

(Offstage helper knocks more loudly.)

Eddie: OK, OK, hold your HORSES! *(Goes to the "door," doing karate chops and kicks on the way.)* Hi-YAH! Hoo-HA! Hi-YAH!

*(**Eddie** opens the "door." **Tracy** enters the stage.)*

Tracy: HI, Eddie! What's going ON?

Eddie: *(Glancing back at the TV)* Oh HI, Tracy. I was just watching *TURBO MORPHIN' DANGER LIZARDS*! *(Does more karate chops and kicks in the direction of **Tracy**.)* Hoo-HA! Hi-YAH!

Tracy: WHOA! Calm DOWN! I didn't come over to do KARATE CHOPS. I came to see whether you'd LEARNED YOUR VERSE yet.

Eddie: Learned my WHAT?

Tracy: For CHURCH, remember? We're supposed to memorize PSALM 119:105.

Eddie: What's THAT?

Tracy: "Your WORD is a LAMP to my FEET and a LIGHT for my PATH" (Psalm 119:105).

Eddie: Man, I could NEVER remember a long verse like THAT!

Tracy: LONG? It's only FOURTEEN WORDS!

Eddie: Plus that "PSALM" part with all those NUMBERS!

Tracy: Hey, it's EASY. I learned it. So TURN OFF the TV, and I'll help you MEMORIZE it.

Eddie: *(Moaning)* OHH, I'll...I'll turn the TV DOWN. *(Walks to the imaginary TV and pushes an imaginary button.)* THERE. *(Returns to stand near **Tracy**, but keeps glancing back to see the TV.)*

Tracy: OK. Now REPEAT AFTER ME: "Your WORD is a LAMP to my FEET...

Eddie: *(Watching TV)* "Your LAMP is a WORD to my FEET...

Tracy: No, no. "Your WORD is a LAMP to my FEET...

Eddie: *(Watching TV)* "My WORD has a CRAMP in its FEET..."

Tracy: EDDIE! You're not paying ATTENTION!

Eddie: *(Watching TV)* SURE I am! It's just that I can't MEMORIZE anything!

Tracy: You can TOO!

Eddie: I can NOT! *(Pauses.)* Hey did you know that the FIRST EPISODE of *Turbo Morphin' Danger Lizards* had a bad guy named OCTOPUS MAN? He was played by RONALD O'TURKEY, a LITTLE-KNOWN actor from TWIN FALLS, IDAHO, whose FIRST stage appearance was in a local production of *SNOW WHITE AND THE SEVEN SEALS*.

Tracy: You don't SAY.

Eddie: But the REALLY interesting thing is that the first episode had a DIFFERENT BEGINNING to the THEME SONG. Instead of saying, "HERE they are, FASTER than a car, PURPLE, ORANGE, SLIGHTLY GREENISH-YELLOW, OFF-WHITE, and GLOW-IN-THE-DARK…" it went, "HERE they are, COMING at you, PURPLE, ORANGE, SLIGHTLY GREENISH-YELLOW, GLOW-IN-THE-DARK, and OFF-WHITE TOO…"

Tracy: I thought you said you COULDN'T MEMORIZE anything.

Eddie: I CAN'T!

Tracy: Uh-HUH. Well, let's try learning the BIBLE VERSE NUMBERS first. REPEAT after ME: PSALM 119:105.

Eddie: (*Watching TV*) Uh…PSALM 19:95.

Tracy: NO! Now try it AGAIN.

Eddie: I just can't memorize NUMBERS! (*Pauses.*) By the WAY, did you know the original OCTOPUS MAN COSTUME weighed FIFTY-SIX POUNDS and had FOUR THOUSAND FIVE HUNDRED AND TWENTY-THREE SUCTION CUPS on it?

Tracy: That's…INCREDIBLE.

Eddie: And you want to know how TALL each of the Turbo Morphin' Danger Lizards is? Purple is SIX FOOT TWO, Orange is FIVE FOOT NINE, Slightly Greenish-Yellow is SIX FOOT FOUR…

Tracy: (*Interrupting*) OK, OK, I give UP, Eddie! It's OBVIOUS that you CAN'T MEMORIZE ANYTHING!

Eddie: YEAH, that's RIGHT. So I guess I'll get back to WATCHING my SHOW, huh?

Tracy: YEP. You wouldn't have wanted that PRIZE for memorizing verses, ANYWAY.

Eddie: PRIZE? WHAT prize?

Tracy: Whoever learns the MOST VERSES gets to choose either a TROPICAL

FISH TANK...

Eddie: UGH!

Tracy: ...or a COMPLETE SET of TURBO MORPHIN' DANGER LIZARDS TRADING CARDS.

Eddie: WHAT? Are you SERIOUS? A complete SET?

Tracy: YEP.

Eddie: MAN! Bring on the VERSES! "Your WORD is a LAMP to my FEET and a LIGHT for my PATH" (Psalm 119:105). "Your WORD is a LAMP to my FEET and a LIGHT for my PATH" (Psalm 119:105).

Tracy: *(Speaking to the audience)* WELL, well. It's a MIRACLE!

Eddie: YEAH! It's like...like a FOG has lifted from my BRAIN! I've got to TURN OFF that TV so I can CONCENTRATE! *(Walks to the TV and pushes a button.)* Where's my BIBLE? I've got to find more VERSES! *(Exits the stage.)*

Tracy: *(Speaking to the audience)* It's AMAZING what the BRAIN can DO...when it WANTS to! *(Exits the stage.)*

● **To Talk About:**

- What three things—other than Bible verses—have you've memorized? How did you learn them?
- Why is it easier for most kids to get excited about a TV show than it is for them to get excited about the Bible?
- Other than winning prizes, what's a good reason for memorizing Bible verses?
- Has knowing a Bible verse or idea ever helped you or someone you know? If so, how?

● **Other Topical Tie-Ins:**

The Bible's importance   Entertainment   Priorities

The Two Little Pigs

Topic: Forgiveness

Scriptures You Might Read: Matthew 5:43-47; Colossians 3:13

The Scene: A land of fairy tales

The Simple Setup: No set is required. Station **Narrator** at an offstage microphone. Rather than trying to dress the performers in elaborate animal costumes, simply encourage them to act like the creatures they represent. **Red** should wear red and carry a basket.

Puppet Options: This skit would be an especially good one to do with puppets. Use pigs for **Pigs 1** and **2**, a dog for **Wolf**, and a girl puppet with a red outfit, if possible for **Red**. If you want puppets and live actors to interact, cast a leader as **Narrator**.

Extra Touches: If you use human actors and have the time, you could have them wear accessories that suggest their animal identities. For example, have **Pigs 1** and **2** wear plastic pig noses with rubber bands, or make noses from cardboard tubes and pink paper. You could also have them wear pig ears made of pink felt or paper glued to headbands. **Wolf** could wear a plastic dog nose with an elastic strap or black paper with tape and floppy ears made of felt secured with bobby pins.

The Characters:
> **Narrator**, who's full of himself or herself
> **Pig 1**, a cranky grudge-holder
> **Pig 2**, a polite forgiver
> **Wolf**, a secretly nice guy
> **Little Red Riding Hood**, a tough and hungry girl

● ● ● ● ● ● ● ●

*(As the skit begins, **Pigs 1** and **2** are standing at center stage.)*

Narrator: And NOW, the story of the TWO LITTLE PIGS.

Pig 1: HEY, shouldn't that be THREE little pigs?

Narrator: SORRY, the BUDGET didn't ALLOW for THREE.

Pig 1: ALWAYS with the BUDGET!

Narrator: *(Clears throat.)* AHEM. ONCE upon a TIME there were TWO LITTLE PIGS. The FIRST little pig built a house of STRAW.

Pig 1: WHAT am I, an IDIOT? Who builds a house out of STRAW? What kind of BUILDING CODES do you people have around here, ANYWAY?

Narrator: The FIRST little pig built a house of STRAW!

Pig 1: All RIGHT, all RIGHT! *(Quickly pantomimes building a house of straw.)* LA dee DA dee DA. Maybe while I'm AT it, I should make myself a TRUCK out of POPCORN!

Narrator: The SECOND little pig built a house of BRICKS.

Pig 2: EXCUSE me, didn't the SECOND little pig build a house of WOOD or STICKS or something?

Narrator: We're SKIPPING that one. BUDGET problems, you know.

Pig 2: Oh, yes. BRICKS it IS. *(Pantomimes building a house of bricks.)* LA dee DA dee DA.

Narrator: Just as they FINISHED building their houses, along came a WOLF.

*(**Wolf** enters the stage.)*

Pig 1: THAT doesn't look like a WOLF! It looks like a DOG!

Narrator: Yes, we KNOW. It's that pesky BUDGET. *(Pauses.)* The WOLF came to the house made of STRAW. And the wolf said...

Wolf: LITTLE PIG, LITTLE PIG, let me come IN!

Narrator: And the FIRST little pig said...

Pig 1: NOT by the HAIR of my CHINNY-CHIN-CHIN! *(Pauses.)* Now just a MINUTE! I don't HAVE any hair on my CHINNY-CHIN-CHIN! I need WHISKERS! *(Calling toward backstage)* MAKEUP!

Narrator: Sorry, we couldn't AFFORD makeup. UNION WAGES, you see. And the wolf said...

Wolf: Then I'll HUFF, and I'll PUFF, and I'll BLOW your house in!

Narrator: *(Speaking as **Wolf** pretends to blow down the imaginary house around **Pig 1**)* So he HUFFED ,and he PUFFED, and he BLEW DOWN the house made of STRAW.

Pig 1: SURPRISE, SURPRISE! And I thought that straw would last FOREVER!

Narrator: And the wolf ATE the first little pig ALL UP.

Pig 1: WHOA! *(Runs to imaginary brick house and stands next to **Pig 2**.)* Let's make sure NO ANIMALS ARE HARMED in the MAKING OF THIS PICTURE!

Narrator: So the wolf came to the house made of BRICKS. And the wolf said...

Wolf: LITTLE PIG, LITTLE PIG, let me come IN!

Narrator: And the SECOND little pig said...

Pig 2: NOT by the HAIR of my CHINNY-CHIN-CHIN! *(**Pig 1** looks at **Pig 2** and shakes head.)* It's OK! I'm IMAGINING I have hair on my chinny-chin-chin. It's called METHOD acting.

Narrator: And the WOLF said...

Wolf: Then I'll HUFF, and I'll PUFF, and I'll BLOW your house in!

Narrator: So he HUFFED, and he PUFFED... *(**Wolf** blows at imaginary house.)* And he HUFFED, and he PUFFED... *(**Wolf** blows again.)* And he HUFFED, and he PUFFED...

*(**Wolf** blows and blows and finally collapses.)*

Wolf: PLEASE, no MORE! We all KNOW how the story goes! I can't blow down a house made of BRICKS! *(Speaking to **Pigs**)* Come ON, now, have a HEART. If I blow any MORE, I'll PASS OUT! Let me into your HOUSE, PLEASE!

Pig 1: What are we, STUPID? WE know what'll happen if we let you in here! You'll EAT US ALL UP! You'll be TAKIN' our BACON!

Wolf: NO! I PROMISE I won't! You're SAFE with me. I've become a VEGETARIAN.

Pig 2: Maybe he's telling the TRUTH. Maybe he WON'T hurt us.

Pig 1: Are you KIDDING? He ALREADY tried to DESTROY our HOMES!

Pig 2: But the STORY said he HAD to. Maybe we should FORGIVE him.

Pig 1: FORGIVE him? And I thought pigs were SMART animals.

Pig 2: We're SUPPOSED to forgive others—even LOVE our ENEMIES! Who

KNOWS, we might even become FRIENDS.

Pig 1: FRIENDS with a WOLF? You'd better lay off the SLOP, pal. It's affecting your BRAIN.

Wolf: PLEASE forgive me. I'd like to be your FRIEND! REALLY!

Pig 2: It's TIME to FORGIVE. I'm going to let him IN. *(Opens imaginary door of brick house.)*

Pig 1: STOP! You're PICKLING our PIG'S FEET! You're SMOKING our SAUSAGES!

*(**Wolf** walks through the "door" **Pig 2** is holding open.)*

Wolf: OOH! NICE PLACE you've got here...even if it IS invisible.

Pig 2: Well, EVERYTHING looks good in BRICK, don't you THINK?

Pig 1: Will you STOP that? We're about to be EATEN!

Wolf: No you're not. I really HAVE quit eating pigs. But if you have some BLUEBERRY GRANOLA, I'd LOVE some of THAT.

Pig 2: Why, I think we have some RIGHT HERE in the INVISIBLE CUPBOARD. *(Pretends to look in imaginary cupboard.)*

*(**Little Red Riding Hood** enters, carrying a basket.)*

Red: WELL, what have we HERE?

Pig 2: It's LITTLE RED RIDING HOOD, that girl who's always walking through the FOREST with a BASKET.

Red: Looks to ME like a house made of BRICKS. If I know my FAIRY TALES, there must be PIGS inside. Some NICE JUICY PIGS! And GRANNY AND I are in the MOOD for PORK CHOPS!

Pig 1: YIPES!

Pig 2: She wants to EAT us!

Wolf: Well, since you guys were NICE enough to FORGIVE me, the LEAST I can do is HELP you OUT. *(Goes to the "door" and opens it.)* HEY, Little RED!

Red: Well, if it isn't the WOLF. What BIG EYES you have, but that's ANOTHER story.

Wolf: I won't let you EAT my FRIENDS, Red.

Red: Is that SO? What a BIG MOUTH you have.

Wolf: All the better to HUFF…and PUFF…and BLOW YOU AWAY! *(Blows long and hard.)*

Red: *(Totters backward as if being pushed by the blast of air.)* AARGH! (**Red** *is "blown" offstage.)*

Pig 1: You DID IT! You really HELPED us!

Pig 2: Looks like FORGIVENESS is a GOOD IDEA, huh?

Wolf: Now if I could have some of that BLUEBERRY GRANOLA…

Pig 2: *(Looking in imaginary cupboard again)* HMM, I THOUGHT we had some, but this is as BARE as MOTHER HUBBARD'S CUPBOARD.

Pig 1: HMPH. A BUDGET problem, no doubt.

Wolf: THAT'S OK. We'll just go to the GROCERY STORE and GET some.

*(**Wolf, Pig 1,** and **Pig 2** start to exit the stage.)*

Pig 1: Uh, shouldn't we be hearing from the NARRATOR about now?

Narrator: NOPE. They CUT THE BUDGET again. I got FIRED.

Pig 1: Too BAD. Well then, I'LL say it: Except for the NARRATOR, they all lived HAPPILY ever AFTER!

(All characters exit the stage.)

● To Talk About:

- Do you think the pigs should have forgiven the wolf? Why or why not?
- What three people have forgiven you the most in your lifetime? Do you think it was difficult or easy for them? Why?
- When it comes to forgiveness, which of the characters in this skit acted the most like God has acted toward you?

● Other Topical Tie-Ins:

Loving your enemies   Prejudice   Making friends

The Unhappy Meal

Topic: Joy

Scriptures You Might Read: Psalm 118:24; Philippians 4:4

The Scene: A fast-food restaurant

The Simple Setup: You'll need a table for the fast-food counter. Put a paper lunch bag under the table, and put something in the bag to give it bulk. **Kid** can wear casual clothes; give **Server** as much of a fast-food restaurant uniform as you can muster—a paper hat or baseball cap and shirt with name tag, for example. Actors of either gender could play both roles, with minor word changes.

Puppet Options: Use puppets for both roles if you like. Or cast a live actor as **Server** if you prefer interaction between puppets and live actors.

Extra Touches: If you wish, make the set look more like a fast-food counter by using a backward bookcase or a row of backward file cabinets to create the illusion of a solid counter. Put up signs with names and prices of fast-food items.

The Characters:
Kid, who's glum and looks tired
Server, who's energetic and streetwise

*(As the skit begins, **Server** is standing behind the counter. **Kid** enters the stage.)*

Server: Welcome to MCDUMBO'S. Can I take your ORDER?

Kid: *(Sighing)* YEAH. I'll have an UNHAPPY MEAL.

Server: UNhappy meal?

Kid: YEAH.

Server: Don't you mean a HAPPY MEAL?

Kid: No, an UNhappy meal.

Server: But WHY would you want an UNhappy meal?

Kid: Because I don't have anything to be HAPPY about.

Server: Why NOT?

Kid: Because I'm a CHRISTIAN.

Server: Oh I SEE. So you're going to LIVE FOREVER; you're FRIENDS with the MOST POWERFUL BEING in the UNIVERSE; and you're on your way to a place where there's NO PAIN, NO SICKNESS, AND NO MATH HOMEWORK.

Kid: RIGHT.

Server: Well, I can SEE why you'd be UNHAPPY. Why, that would almost give me a HEADACHE.

Kid: So can I have an UNHAPPY MEAL?

Server: Are you KIDDING? What have you got to be unhappy ABOUT?

Kid: Um, all the stuff I CAN'T DO. Like, I can't take DRUGS...

Server: YEAH...

Kid: Can't get DRUNK...

Server: YEAH...

Kid: Can't play with HAND GRENADES...

Server: Boy, that's a TOUGH one. You MUST be miserable.

Kid: So can I have my UNHAPPY MEAL?

Server: You're UNHAPPY because you can't do things that might get you ARRESTED, SICK, or DEAD?

Kid: Well, when you put it THAT way...

Server: SEE? What you want is a HAPPY meal! Will that be with the BURGER or the CHICKEN?

Kid: You don't UNDERSTAND. I HAVE to have an UNhappy meal. Christians aren't SUPPOSED to be happy.

Server: How do you KNOW?

Kid: Well, old Mr. FURPLE at CHURCH never SMILES.

Server: Maybe his TEETH don't fit.

Kid: And Mrs. VEEPLE—SHE always looks like she just SUCKED on a LEMON.

Server: Maybe she DID.

Kid: So I'll take that UNHAPPY MEAL now, if you don't MIND.

Server: Hold ON. Does it say somewhere in the BIBLE that you're not supposed to be happy?

Kid: Um, I'm sure it MUST.

Server: WHERE?

Kid: I don't KNOW! I don't READ the Bible very much, OK?

Server: Why NOT?

Kid: I might accidentally ENJOY it.

Server: (Sighs.) I give UP.

Kid: Now about that UNHAPPY MEAL…

Server: SORRY. We only have HAPPY meals.

Kid: Well, could you take a HAPPY meal and HOLD the HAPPINESS?

Server: NO. But I'll tell you what I CAN do. I can give you a BURGER with STUFF YOU DON'T LIKE ON IT. I can give you COLD FRIES. I can put TOO MUCH WATER in your POP. And for the TOY, I can give you a SMELLY OLD SOCK somebody left in the LOST AND FOUND.

Kid: OK.

(**Server** rummages under counter and comes up with a paper bag.)

Server: Here's your UNHAPPY MEAL. That'll be NINETEEN DOLLARS AND FORTY-TWO CENTS.

Kid: WHAT?

Server: Hey, I'm OVERCHARGING you. I figured it would make you more... UNHAPPY.

Kid: Oh. THANKS.

(**Kid** pantomimes giving money to **Server**, takes bag, and starts to leave.)

Server: So... are you HAPPY now?

Kid: YES. I mean, NO. I mean... UH-OH! (Speaking to self) I'm not SUPPOSED to be HAPPY. But if I'm UNhappy, does that mean I should feel HAPPY about it? Or maybe I should TRY to be HAPPY, which would make me more UNhappy... (Still mumbling, exits the stage.)

Server: HEY, have a GOOD... I mean, have a BAD DAY! (Shrugs and exits the stage.)

● **To Talk About:**

- Have you ever gotten the idea that Christians aren't supposed to have a good time? If so, how?
- What have you done that's been the most fun ever? Do you think that when Jesus was your age, he would have enjoyed it? Why or why not?
- Do you think following Jesus gives you any reasons to be happy? Can you name two that weren't mentioned in the skit?
- Read Proverbs 17:22. How would you write this message in your own words on a "cheer up" greeting card for the kid in the skit?

● **Other Topical Tie-Ins:**

Christians and fun   Reasons to follow Jesus   Being thankful

Virtual Reality

Topic: Taking Care of Your Body

Scriptures You Might Read: Psalm 139:13-14; 1 Corinthians 6:19-20

The Scene: A bedroom

The Simple Setup: You'll need a chair at center stage and a "virtual pet," which could be anything that looks like a small electronic device as long as you don't mind it being stepped on and as long as a string can be attached to it. You'll also need a six-foot length of string and a bag of marshmallows. Put a blanket in a large basket (the kind a dog or cat might sleep in), place the basket at stage left or right, and put the virtual pet in it. The **Voice** should speak into an offstage microphone; the crunching sound can be created there, too, by cracking walnuts with a nutcracker.

Puppet Options: You could use puppets for **Erin** and **Brianna**. If **Erin** is a puppet, fasten the string to the virtual pet ahead of time. You probably can dispense with the chair, too. If you prefer to have puppets interact with live actors, cast a leader or child as **Brianna**.

Extra Touches: If you'd like, add an electronic beep at the offstage microphone each time **Erin** pushes a button.

The Characters:
      Erin, an exhausted girl
      Brianna, her level-headed friend
      Voice of Virtual Varmint, the mechanical-sounding voice of a "virtual pet"

*(As the skit begins, **Erin** is slumped in a chair at center stage, sleeping. **Brianna** enters the stage and looks around.)*

Brianna: ERIN? ERIN, are you HERE? Your MOM said you were… *(Sees **Erin**.)* ERIN? Are you ASLEEP? It's the MIDDLE of the DAY!

Erin: *(Waking)* HUH? WHAT? Oh HI, Brianna. Guess I DOZED OFF again.

Brianna: Erin, I haven't seen you around for a WHOLE MONTH! Where have you BEEN?

Erin: Uh…right HERE, I guess.

Brianna: You've been in your ROOM for a MONTH? How COME?

Erin: Um...I've been...BUSY.

Brianna: BUSY? Busy with WHAT?

Erin: Well...

Voice: I require ATTENTION!

Brianna: What was THAT?

Voice: I require ATTENTION!

Brianna: Who said THAT?

Erin: *(Wearily getting up)* That's V.V.

Brianna: Who's V.V.?

Erin: VIRTUAL VARMINT.

Brianna: VIRTUAL VARMINT? Who's THAT?

Erin: *(Trudging across stage toward the basket)* It's my VIRTUAL PET. YOU know, one of those ELECTRONIC things. It TELLS you whenever it NEEDS something.

Brianna: And what does it need right NOW?

Voice: I require ATTENTION!

*(**Erin** picks up the virtual pet from the basket and examines it.)*

Erin: HMM. It needs FOOD.

Voice: FEED me!

Brianna: FEED me? How can you FEED a MACHINE?

Erin: *(Pushing a "button")* You PUSH this BUTTON. First you CHOOSE the FOOD.

Voice: Not THAT kind! I want TUNA FISH!

Erin: OK! There's TUNA FISH!

Voice: And I want MUSTARD on it!

Erin: MUSTARD? All right. *(Pushing another button)* There's MUSTARD.

Voice: Yum, YUM.

Erin: THERE! Now leave me ALONE for five minutes! *(Trudges back to the chair.)*

Voice: BURP!

Brianna: Oh, GROSS!

Erin: *(Sitting heavily)* So BRIANNA, what is it LIKE in the OUTSIDE WORLD?

Brianna: It's BEAUTIFUL! SUNNY! I was thinking maybe we could go on a HIKE.

Erin: Oh, I CAN'T. Got to take care of V.V.

Brianna: Erin, you look AWFUL! You've got to get OUT of here and get some FRESH AIR and EXERCISE.

Erin: Too TIRED.

Brianna: That VIRTUAL VARMINT has taken over your LIFE! You need to...

Voice: *(Interrupting)* I require ATTENTION!

Brianna: Not AGAIN! How often does it DO this?

Erin: *(Getting up and trudging to the basket)* Every MINUTE or so, TWENTY-FOUR HOURS A DAY.

Brianna: You're KIDDING! How do you SLEEP?

Erin: I DON'T.

Voice: Take me for a WALK.

Erin: OK, OK. I'll TAKE you for a walk.

Brianna: HOW do you take VIRTUAL VARMINT for a WALK?

Erin: Like THIS. *(Attaches a string to the virtual pet and begins to walk in a circle, dragging the pet on the floor.)*

Brianna: HUH. Well, we can at least do that OUTSIDE, CAN'T we?

Erin: Oh, NO. V.V. doesn't LIKE fresh air.

Voice: FASTER! Walk me FASTER!

Erin: OK, OK! *(Walks faster in a circle.)*

Voice: FASTER! Walk me FASTER!

*(**Erin** walks faster and faster but soon runs out of breath.)*

Erin: Can't...keep...this...UP...*(Stops walking.)* Maybe if I have something to EAT, I'll get enough ENERGY. *(Picks up a bag of marshmallows.)* I'll just eat this bag of MARSHMALLOWS.

Brianna: MARSHMALLOWS? THOSE aren't HEALTHY! Have some FRUIT or a SANDWICH.

Erin: No TIME for that. MARSHMALLOWS are QUICK.

Brianna: Erin, LOOK at you! You're not getting any SLEEP, you're not getting any FRESH AIR, you're EATING the WRONG FOODS, you're wearing yourself OUT waiting on that...that MACHINE.

Voice: I require ATTENTION!

Brianna: Don't LISTEN to it, Erin! You've got to take CARE of yourself. GOD made your BODY, and he wants you to CARE for it.

Voice: I require ATTENTION!

Erin: But I've got to take care of V.V.

Voice: Put me on the CHAIR! *(**Erin** rushes to do so.)* No, put me on the FLOOR! *(**Erin** rushes to do so.)* No, feed me a bag of MARSHMALLOWS! *(**Erin** picks up bag.)* No, put me on the CEILING!

Erin: On the CEILING? How am I supposed to do THAT? You stupid MACHINE! You're nothing more than a TALKING CALCULATOR! You're RUINING my LIFE! *(Suddenly stamps on the virtual pet, then jumps up and down on it.)*

(Offstage helper makes crunching sound effect.)

Voice: *(Speaking quickly in a high-pitched voice like a tape speeding up)* I require attention! I require attention! *(Speaking slowly in a low-pitched voice like a tape grinding to a halt)* I...require...ATTENTION...

*(**Erin** collapses, exhausted, in the chair.)*

Brianna: ERIN, you DID it! You're FREE! You're not a SLAVE anymore!

Erin: BRIANNA?

Brianna: YES?

Erin: I think...I require...ATTENTION.

Brianna: I think so, TOO. *(Helping **Erin** to her feet)* Let's go take care of that BODY of yours, OK?

*(**Brianna**, still supporting **Erin**, exits the stage with **Erin**.)*

Voice: *(Speaking slowly in a low-pitched voice)* Ooh...that...SMARTS.

● **To Talk About:**

- Do you think most kids in your school take good care of their bodies? Why or why not?
- How could the following machines have a bad effect on children's health?
  - a TV
  - a computer
  - a car
  - a toaster oven?
- Why do you suppose God gave us bodies—why not have us float around without them?
- Which of the following do you think would make the biggest difference in our group: getting more exercise or cutting down on junk food? Next time we get together, how could we include both of these in our plans?

● **Other Topical Tie-Ins:**

Self-esteem   Living a balanced life   God's creation

Warning Labels

Topic: Entertainment Choices

Scriptures You Might Read: Psalm 119:37; Philippians 4:8

The Scene: A superstore

The Simple Setup: No set is required; and actors should pantomime use of any props. Have **Announcer** deliver his or her lines from an offstage microphone. **Kids 1** and **2** may wear casual clothes.

Puppet Options: Use puppets for **Kids 1** and **2** if you prefer. If you want to mix puppets and live actors, cast a child or leader as **Kid 1**.

Extra Touches: If you'd like, dress up the stage with some "sale" signs to help identify the setting.

The Characters:

    Kid 1, who's innocent and easily impressed

    Kid 2, who's supposedly cool and sophisticated

    Announcer, an enthusiastic offstage voice

*(As the skit begins, **Kids 1** and **2** enter the stage, looking around as if at a huge room.)*

Kid 1: WOW! I can't believe we're finally at HUMONGO-MART!

Kid 2: The store that has EVERYTHING…and MORE!

Announcer: ATTENTION, Humongo-Mart shoppers! Now on aisle SEVEN, pink and green striped LIGHT BULBS are only SEVENTY-NINE CENTS EACH!

Kid 2: SEE? They've got EVERYTHING!

Kid 1: Let's go to the ENTERTAINMENT department. I bet they've got some GREAT stuff THERE.

*(**Kids 1** and **2** pantomime walking.)*

Announcer: ATTENTION, Humongo-Mart shoppers! On aisle FIFTEEN, CREAMED LIZARD GIZZARDS are just $2.59 a CAN!

Kid 2: LIZARD GIZZARDS? I'd rather watch these TV SETS. There must be a HUNDRED of 'em!

Kid 1: Now THAT'S ENTERTAINMENT! *(Pauses.)* Uh, what program are they showing?

Kid 2: Oh that's *JERKY STRINGER*.

Kid 1: You mean the program in which they CALL EACH OTHER NASTY NAMES and BREAK CHAIRS OVER EACH OTHER'S HEADS?

Kid 2: YEP! Sometimes they have to BLEEP OUT the WHOLE SHOW.

Kid 1: But this show is rated TV-14. WE'RE not supposed to WATCH it.

Kid 2: Oh those LABELS don't mean ANYTHING. This stuff is GOOD for you!

Announcer: ATTENTION, Humongo-Mart shoppers! Now on aisle THIRTY-NINE, you'll find BEDROOM SLIPPERS FOR HAMSTERS, sizes SMALL, EXTRA small, MEDIUM, EXTRA medium small, LARGE small EXTRA medium, and VERY BIG INDEED—ONLY $5.99 a PAIR!

Kid 1: Boy, that *JERKY STRINGER* is SOME SHOW! But I'd rather RENT A VIDEO. Do they HAVE videos here?

Announcer: ATTENTION, Humongo-Mart shoppers! On aisle SEVENTY-TWO you'll find our HOTTEST VIDEO RENTAL, *SKELETON BABY SITTERS, 13!* It'll CHILL you to the BONE! Rated R!

Kid 2: OOH, that sounds GOOD!

Kid 1: But it's rated R!

Kid 2: Those LABELS don't mean ANYTHING. This stuff is GOOD for you!

Announcer: ATTENTION, Humongo-Mart shoppers! Now on aisle NINETY-EIGHT, get the latest sensation for your PAYSTATION GAME SYSTEM! It's *BRAIN CHOPPER WARS*! Or pick the top-selling SOFTWARE for your PC, *INSANE, EVIL, KILLER MANIACS*! YOUR CHOICE, only $59.99!

Kid 2: FORGET the video! THERE'S what you need!

Kid 1: But those games have WARNING LABELS about VIOLENCE, GORE, BLOOD, AND GUTS…

Kid 2: Those LABELS don't mean ANYTHING. This stuff is GOOD for you!

Kid 1: Hey, LOOK! There's a COMPUTER that's hooked up to the INTERNET!

Kid 2: Let's do a little SURFIN', dude! *(Using an imaginary computer mouse)* We'll go to one of my FAVORITE WEB SITES.

Kid 1: *(Looking at an imaginary screen)* WHOA! It says "ADULTS ONLY"!

Kid 2: Those LABELS don't mean ANYTHING. This stuff is GOOD for you!

Announcer: ATTENTION, Humongo-Mart shoppers! Now on aisle 331, from master RAPPERS, 2SCUZZY4WORDS, it's the new CD *BEACH BLANKETY BINGO!* Note PARENTAL WARNING: This album contains OFFENSIVE LYRICS!

Kid 2: HEY, I've heard that album is really GOOD!

Kid 1: But that WARNING about the LANGUAGE...

Kid 2: Those LABELS don't mean ANYTHING. This stuff is GOOD for you!

Kid 1: Well, I'll decide LATER. First let's get something to EAT. This place has FOOD, right?

Kid 2: SURE! Over HERE!

Kid 1: HMM. I'll get this SANDWICH. *(Picks up an imaginary sandwich and turns it over.)* OOPS! The DATE on this sandwich is THREE WEEKS AGO! It's too OLD!

Kid 2: Hey, those LABELS don't mean ANYTHING. This stuff is GOOD for you!

Kid 1: Well...OK.

Kid 2: And something to DRINK. How about this BLUE STUFF in the BOTTLE?

Kid 1: That's SHAMPOO! You can't DRINK it! SEE? The BACK says, "For EXTERNAL use ONLY"!

Kid 2: Those LABELS don't mean ANYTHING. This stuff is GOOD for you!

Kid 1: Well, if you SAY so. I'll just PAY for it. *(Pantomimes taking money from pocket and paying imaginary clerk.)*

Kid 2: Can I have a BITE of your SANDWICH?

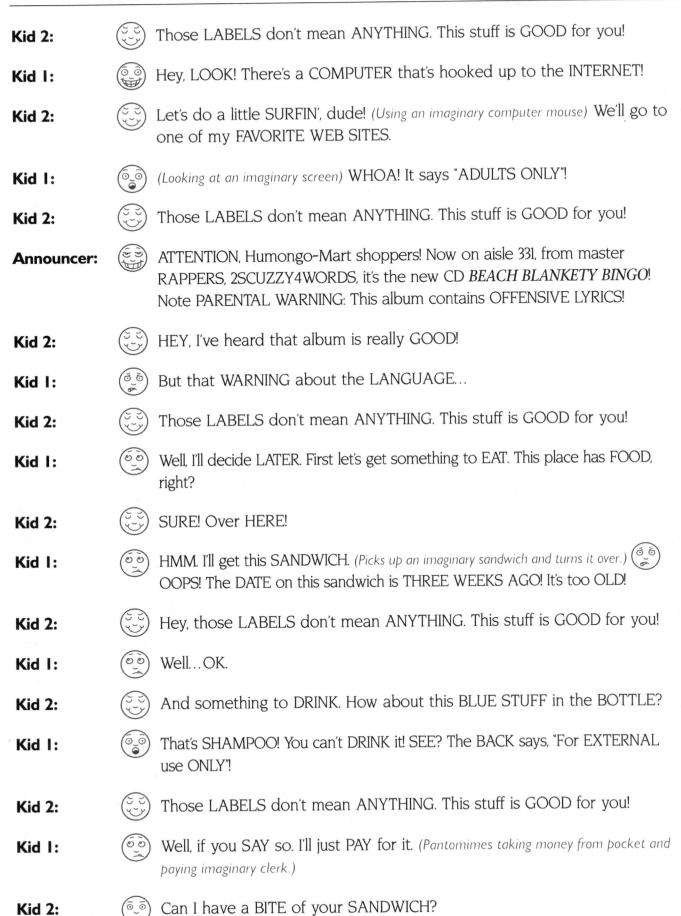

Kid 1: Sure. *(Pantomimes giving half of a sandwich to **Kid 2**. Both take a bite of imaginary sandwich.)* Uh, this tastes kind of FUNNY.

Kid 2: YEAH. Let's WASH IT DOWN with the BLUE stuff. *(They pantomime taking drinks from an imaginary bottle.)*

Kid 1: EEW! I...I think I'm going to be SICK.

Kid 2: I think I'm ALREADY sick!

(They put their hands over their mouths and run off the stage.)

Announcer: ATTENTION, Humongo-Mart shoppers! Now on aisle 762, it's the perfect remedy for that UPSET STOMACH! New POPTO-FIZZMOL, only 4.99! Use only as DIRECTED! And REMEMBER, at HUMONGO-MART, all our stuff is...GOOD for you!

● To Talk About:

- How is watching a video or listening to a song like eating? How is it different?
- What are some "warning labels" you've seen in the Bible or heard at church? Do you pay attention to them? Why or why not?
- Can you name a TV show, Internet Web site, or video game that's fun and good for you?
- How can you know what "stuff" is really "good for you"?

● Other Topical Tie-Ins:

Peer pressure   Listening to wisdom   God's commands

Topics at a Glance

Scripture Index